MASTER POTTERS OF THE INDUSTRIAL REVOLUTION

The Gerverot Beaker

Bevis Hillier

MASTER POTTERS OF THE INDUSTRIAL REVOLUTION

The Turners of Lane End

Cory, Adams & Mackay

First published 1965 by Cory, Adams & Mackay Ltd, 39 Sloane Street, London, S.W.1
Printed and made in Great Britain by W. & J. Mackay & Co Ltd, Chatham

Contents

To My Parents

Acknowledgements

My first obligation is to Mr Reginald Haggar, to whose works of enthusiastic scholarship all students of pottery and the Potteries are indebted. He generously gave me access to the results of his searches through the files of the *Staffordshire Advertiser* and other local newspapers, told me of the Abbott Papers, and read the proofs of this book.

My friend Philip Mansergh translated into English long passages of German prose relating to Louis-Victor Gerverot, and gave further help in interpreting the economics of the Turner-Abbott partnership and of the Industrial Revolution.

Mr George Eyre Stringer, author of a book on New Hall porcelain which contains much information on the Turners, gave me encouragement from the start, and as a potter himself (he was the last managing director of the New Hall factory) was able to give practical information on clays and ceramic processes.

Mrs Elsie Young, a great-great-granddaughter of John Turner I, allowed me to have photographs taken of her fine collection of Turner pottery, and forgave me for leaving her china cabinet in Babylonish confusion.

I am much indebted also to the following:

Mr Jack Barker, Mr Geoffrey Bemrose, Mr David Bindman, Mr Harry Buten, Sir Philip Colfox, Mr and Mrs J. K. des Fontaines, Mr Geoffrey Godden, Mrs Constance Hare, the Rev. Dudley Hodges, Mr Harold Holdway, Miss M. Holmes and Miss M. Ory of the Dorset Record Office, Major and Mrs F. A. Hopkins, Miss Dorothy Hunter, Mrs Jessie Katz, Mr A. J. B. Kiddell, Mr C. O. Langley, Mr John Mallet, Mr A. R. Mountford, Herr Willibald Netto, Mr Nicholas Orme, Mr Eric Plunkett, Mr Alexandre Raghinsky, Mr Cyril Staal, the late Major W. Tapp, Mr Donald Towner, Mr David Lea Turner, Miss Fanny Turner, Sir John Wedgwood, Mr H. Weinberg, and the curators and officials of many British and American museums.

Books consulted are acknowledged in the text and notes, but I should like to express my especial indebtedness to an unpublished thesis, *The Economic Development of the North Staffordshire Potteries since 1730, with Special Reference to the Industrial Revolution,* by Dr John Thomas, lodged in the Senate House of the University of London. Dr Thomas kindly read my proofs.

CHAPTER ONE

Brewood and Stoke

Talking about the Potteries with me, Billy Bennett told me that his father had once pointed out to him, that no potting firm, except Wedgwoods, had survived to the third generation. The first generation was of the people, industrial, simple; the second, though raised in the social grade, was still plodding and energetic and kept the business together; the third was a generation of wastrels coming to grief.

(Arnold Bennett, *Journal*, 26 May 1901)

AT FIRST SIGHT this nutshell history of the decline of a potting dynasty seems to fit the Turners of Lane End to perfection. First came John Turner (1738–87), a simple man devoted to his trade; his sons William (1762–1835) and John (1766–1824) were unremarkable country gentlemen who continued the business; the third generation contained two playboys who were drowned while yachting on the Mediterranean, and a third brother, finding his Staffordshire wife disagreeable, contracted a bigamous marriage in London.

The analogy breaks down, however, when we discover that John Turner I was himself a squireen; that the failure of the business was the result not of feckless behaviour but of losses in the French Revolution; and that the so-called wastrel generation included a perfectly meritorious pharmacist, who lived at Lane End and might have maintained the potting interests had there been any left to maintain.

John Turner I was the son of a lawyer who lived at Brewood Hall, Staffordshire.[1] Brewood is a village about half-way between Stafford and Wolverhampton. The Hall (Plate 1c), a late seventeenth-century building, stands on the eastern outskirts of the village, on the site of a medieval building once occupied by the Fowke family. Towards the end of the nineteenth century the house was 'restored' by two old ladies, the Misses Monckton. As an exercise in philistinism this attempt to convert a seventeenth-century mansion into an Evangelical ranch was something of a *tour de force*. A veranda and stained-glass windows were added. The topiary gardens, which Dr Plot, in 1686, had ranked with those of Hampton Court,[2] were uprooted. Finally, as part of an ancient feud with the Fowke family,

1

the heraldic fleurs-de-lis which surmounted the gateposts were consigned to the kitchen garden.[3] The interior, however, still retains some seventeenth-century panelling and a handsome staircase of the same date. The veranda has been taken down.

Brewood Hall descended in the Turner family to John Turner's grandson, Henry Turner, another lawyer, who, some time after 1853, gave up the house and moved with his family to Wolverhampton, where he had his business.[4] The present owner of Brewood Hall, Major C. O. Langley, is also a lawyer with offices in Wolverhampton.

John Turner I was born in 1738. We know nothing of his early life or education, but we can surmise that he was an educated man. His recipe books, now lost, but still existing in the last century,[5] were written in French to guard against piracy. According to one late source, the actual writing was done by his wife, but we must assume that Turner could read his own recipe books. Probably he attended Brewood Grammar School, though there are no school registers dating from that period.[6] The Hall is near the school, and Turner's father was of precisely that professional class from whose sons most of the school's pupils were drawn. We know, also, that the Turners later had business dealings with the Giffard family of Chillington, with which the school, since its foundation in 1553, had been, and still is, pre-eminently associated. When Thomas Giffard married Charlotte, second daughter of Viscount Courtenay, in 1788, the Turners made them a dinner service painted with their coats of arms. One plate of it is in the British Museum; another, in the collection of Mr Donald Towner, is illustrated in Plate 27a. It is significant that when, ten years earlier, Frances, *first* daughter of Lord Courtenay, had married Sir John Honeywood, their service, similarly decorated, of which also a specimen plate is in the British Museum, was made not by the Turners but by Wedgwood.[7] This suggests that the Turners owed the commission to a Giffard connexion. On the other hand, it might merely be an illustration of what we know to be true—that the Turner factory gained in reputation between 1778 and 1788: in 1784 John Turner was appointed Potter to the Prince of Wales.

Brewood Grammar School was an excellent establishment. Between 1731 and 1745 it came under the direction of an outstanding headmaster, the Rev. William Budworth, Vicar of Brewood. Budworth, who is commemorated by a column of the *Dictionary of National Biography*, was described by his most eminent pupil, Dr Richard Hurd,[8] Bishop of Worcester, as 'a most excellent person', who 'possessed every talent of a perfect institutor of youth, in a degree which, I believe, has rarely been found in any of that profession since the days of Quinctilian [*sic*]'.[9]

Dr Johnson, who had met Budworth in a school at Market Bosworth, and there formed a high opinion of his abilities, applied to him in 1736 for the job of usher at the Grammar School, but was regretfully refused, as Budworth, according to Boswell, thought Johnson's paralytic affliction 'might become the object of imitation or of ridicule, among his pupils'.[10] The succession of Budworth, in 1745, by the usher whom he in fact appointed, the Rev. Roger Bromley, suggests the pleasing speculation that, but for his convulsions, Dr Johnson might have been John Turner's headmaster. Perhaps it was as well for Turner that he was not: some of Johnson's views on education were less than enlightened, and his attempts to apply them were failures.

We do not know what caused John Turner to become a potter. More than a century has elapsed since anyone knew the answer. The sources have dried up. Mr Stringer suggests that some legal contact of Lawyer Turner with the Potteries may have determined the son's career,[11] and colour is given to this speculation by the fact that the Stafford Assizes served both Brewood and the Potteries, being about half-way between the two, so that Turner's father might have made the acquaintance of various potters. John Turner was apprenticed, on 25 March 1753, to Daniel Bird, 'earth potter', of Penkhull, Stoke, for the sum of £20.[12] Bird is a potter of whom little is known. The late W. B. Honey makes a joke about his name, but says nothing further about him.[13] Apparently he did not mark his wares, so there is no piece of pottery that we can with certainty ascribe to him. In spite of this, he has a certain reputation as an innovator. Shaw tells us that he was called 'the flint potter':[14] he was the first to ascertain the exact quantity of flint required by the various kinds of clay to prevent them from cracking in the kiln. In his *Chemistry of Pottery* (1837), Shaw wrote:

> The employment of the Devonshire pipe-clay, by Twyford and Astbury of Shelton, supplied the *white dipped* and the *white stone-ware*; from which the transition was easy to the *flint ware*, by Daniel Bird of Stoke. . . .[15]

According to Shaw, Bird 'made Agate buttons, Knife Hafts, and Flint ware, salt glaze, by which he speedily realised a handsome fortune'.[16] In the Schreiber Collection in the Victoria and Albert Museum there is an agate-glaze jug marked TURNER, the only recorded example of variegated Turner pottery (Plate II). It is described as follows in the Schreiber Collection catalogue of 1885:

> 1186 JUG: the lip and handle terminating in leaves moulded in low relief, marbled brown, yellow and slate blue, to imitate agate. Mark, impressed, TURNER. H. 5½ in.

Turner's apprenticeship was to have lasted five years. In fact, it lasted for less than one year, for in November 1753 Bird was killed.[17] The next we hear of Turner he has set up business himself. Henry Wedgwood wrote, in 1879:

> I am informed by an aged potter that Turner first started to manufacture at the Black Dump, Shelton. The gentleman from whom I received this information stated that he learnt it from Simeon Shaw himself. It is not, however, in Shaw's work, though the author may have added this to his stock of knowledge subsequently to his work being published.[18]

Shaw's printed version is that Turner, in partnership with a Mr R. Banks, began potting in Stoke in 1756, on the site of what is now the Spode-Copeland factory.[19] William was, in fact, the Christian name of Turner's partner, as we learn from old deeds in the Spode-Copeland factory museum; his surname was variously spelt Banks, Bankes, and Bancks.

Two other potters, later more or less eminent in their own right, were employed at the factory: Josiah Spode (previously apprenticed, like Josiah Wedgwood, to Thomas Whieldon)[20] and Charles Harvey.[21] When Turner moved to Lane End in 1759 Banks carried on the Stoke works with Spode as his manager. On 16 October 1775 Banks sold the factory to Jeremiah Smith of Great Fenton (High Sheriff of Staffordshire in 1762), whose son, John Smith (1766–1840), who also became High Sheriff, in 1816, was to marry Turner's youngest daughter, Elizabeth, in 1801.[22] Spode purchased the works from Jeremiah Smith on 29 February 1776. There are two photographs of these old works in Arthur Hayden's *Spode and His Successors* (1925).[23] By that date they had been demolished, but they were still standing in 1879, when Henry Wedgwood wrote:

> The site of the (Turner) manufactory is now covered by the large works of Messrs Copeland. However, the little place has only been incorporated, and may still be seen as complete, with its square and workshops, as when it stood once in the open, and is now devoted to the printing department.[24]

According to Shaw, Turner and Banks made 'white stoneware' at the Stoke factory.[25] Now, it has sometimes been assumed that what Shaw meant by this was the fine, almost porcellanous stoneware for which Turner is best known—the material from which the wares shown in Plates 11–26 were made. But, in fact, Turner did not discover the Green Dock clay from which this fine stoneware was made until about 1780.[26] The Turner moulds which are preserved at the Spode-Copeland factory museum (Plate 13) and which were undoubtedly used on the fine stoneware, were not left behind by Turner when he moved to Lane End in 1759; they were bought up by Spode at the sale of the Turner moulds in 1829.[27]

Mrs Eric Young, John Turner's great-great-granddaughter, has inherited the family collection of Turner pottery. It includes a few examples of white *salt-glaze* stoneware (Plates 2b and 3b). In 1756 Josiah Wedgwood, eight years older than Turner, was still in partnership with Thomas Whieldon, and manufacturing the characteristic Whieldon wares. In an essay on Wedgwood's association with Whieldon, Mr A. T. Morley Hewitt writes:

> Wedgwood in his MSS. states that 'white stoneware' (salt glaze) was the principal article of 'our manufacture'.[28]

It therefore seems reasonable to suggest that Turner and Banks also made white salt-glaze stoneware—a suggestion strengthened by the knowledge that Turner's master, Bird, made salt-glaze and that the earliest dated example of Turner pottery, the Degg teapot (Plate 2a), made only a few years after Turner moved to Lane End, is, if not itself salt-glaze, of moulded salt-glaze type.

According to Simeon Shaw, it was in 1762 that Turner moved to Lane End.[29] In 1759, however, when an Act was obtained for erecting turnpikes on the road from Derby to Newcastle-under-Lyme, one of the trustees for the Staffordshire area was 'John Turner, Lane End'.[30] On 15 October 1759, when he was married to Ann Emery, daughter of William Emery, a Brewood timber merchant, he was described in the parish register as 'John Turner of the parish of Stoke in the County of Stafford, potter'. Lane End had no church of its own until 1762, and was part of the parish of Stoke. So Turner may have been in either place in October, but was certainly at Lane End by the end of 1759. Possibly he moved after his marriage into a new house and a new factory.

NOTES TO CHAPTER ONE

[1] R. G. Haggar, *Staffordshire Chimney Ornaments* (1955), p. 51; G. E. Stringer, *New Hall Porcelain* (1949), p. 18; M. E. Wakefield, *Brewood* (1959), p. 82.

[2] '. . . pleasant *walks* and *Topiary* works; for the latter whereof *Laurembergius* notes that the English are as expert as most *Nations*, quoting *Hampton-Court* as remarkable for them: and so is *Brewood-Hall* the seat of *Mr Ferrers Fowk* of this *County*, where in the *whitethorn* hedg between the *Garden* and *Court* before the house, there are several *Animals*, *Castles*, &c. formed *arte Topiaria*, not unlike those ingraven by *Laurembergius*.' (Dr Robert Plot, *History of Staffordshire*, 1686, pp. 380–1.)

³ The fleur-de-lis was part of the Fowke coat of arms. The arms granted to Bartholomew Fowke in 1580 were: Azure, a fleur-de-lis argent; on a chief indented of the second a lion passant gules. The arms of John Fowke, Lord Mayor of London in 1653, were: Vert, a fleur-de-lis argent.

Mrs M. E. Wakefield, in the chapter of her book on Brewood entitled 'A Great Brewood Potter', makes this suggestion: 'The Turners' pottery mark was a crown with a fleur-de-lis under it. This is evidently a reminiscence of Brewood Hall, where the fleur-de-lis in stone was on either gatepost' (p. 82). But, in fact, the emblem used by the Turners represented the Prince of Wales's feathers, and was used by them after John Turner's appointment as Potter to the Prince of Wales in 1784.

Curiously enough, the Fowke fleur-de-lis *was* later used as a pottery mark, at the Leicestershire factory of Lowesby, founded by Sir Frederick Gustavus Fowke in 1835. (See Alfred Billson, *Lowesby and its Pottery*, in *The Connoisseur*, June 1907, p. 77.)

⁴ Henry Turner (1809–78) was the son of John Turner II. He moved into Brewood Hall after the death of his father's widow in 1840, having previously lived at Dean's End, Brewood, as an attorney and agent to the Atlas Fire Office. When exactly he moved to Wolverhampton is not certain. His daughters were listed among the donors to a new church at Bishop's Wood, Brewood, on 16 June 1850, consecrated in 1851, and their address was given as Brewood Hall. (They contributed £20.) They did not, however, subscribe to a new church at Coven in 1857, or to the new National School at Brewood in 1859, and this may be an indication that the family had by then left the district (William Parke, *Notes and Collections relating to Brewood*, 1860, Supplement, pp. 4, 6–7, 8–9). White's *Gazeteer of Staffordshire*, 1851, records that '*Brewood Hall*, formerly the seat of the Fowke family, is now the residence of Mr H. Turner, solicitor' (p. 446). He is also listed as an attorney in Darlington Street, Wolverhampton (p. 111). Evidently Turner was still in Brewood in 1853, for in that year he was engaged in acrimonious litigation over some land in Brewood, and claimed the advantage over his opponent that he was an inhabitant of the village. From this lawsuit, to which Chapter V of Douglas Thompson's *History of Brewood Grammar School* (1953) is devoted, Henry Turner emerges as a scurrilous and unlikeable man. Certainly the Turners must have left the Hall by 23 September 1869, for on that date, according to the parish register, Leonora Monckton died there. (The Hall remained in the Monckton family until bought by the present owner in 1930.) Henry Turner died in Wolverhampton in August 1878, and was buried at Brewood.

⁵ In an article on the Turners in the *Staffordshire Sentinel* of 8 February 1879, Henry Wedgwood wrote: 'His [John Turner I's] book of recipes, which was long in the hands of Mr H. Palmer, but lost in some unaccountable manner, showed how exact our potter was in all his trials of bodies and experiments. That he was a man of culture is proved from the fact that all his recipes and marginal notes on their working, were written in French.' But in 1894 Henry Palmer, a great-grandson of John Turner I, sent some of the family collection of Turner wares for exhibition at the Imperial Institute, London, and in an interview recorded in the *Staffordshire Evening Post* of 18 May 1894 he made a statement which contradicts that of Henry Wedgwood: 'Major Palmer said he had one of two books, both of which he had formerly possessed, which the old man used for the purpose of recording all

II. Pearl ware jug with 'agate' glaze. Mark: TURNER impressed. (See p. 3.) (Victoria and Albert Museum.)

his experiments and receipts. The book is written by his wife in French, the object evidently being to avoid the risk of workmen or others benefiting by his investigations and hard-earned knowledge. The other book was of the same sort, but larger than the one now in Major Palmer's possession, and he expressed the belief that it had been lent to someone and lost sight of. At all events, it had disappeared from his custody.' Mrs Eric Young, the daughter of Major Palmer, who has inherited the family collection of Turner pottery, does not know what has become of the recipe book, or whether its companion was ever recovered.

[6] *Ex. inf.* J. Finney, Esq., Headmaster of Brewood Grammar School, letter of 16 November 1962.

[7] The two services, Turner and Wedgwood, are discussed in the *Transactions* of the English Ceramic Circle, vol. iv, part 5, p. 58.

[8] Richard Hurd, b. 1719, son of John Hurd (1685–1755), a Brewood farmer. Fellow of Emmanuel College, Cambridge, 1742. Bishop of Lichfield, 1774. Bishop of Worcester, 1781. Offered Archbishopric of Canterbury by George III, but refused it 'as a charge not suited to his temper or talents'. Died 1808.

On 6 December 1773 Wedgwood wrote to his partner Bentley that Lady Littleton (wife of Sir Edward Littleton, who had been at school with Hurd under Budworth) wished to make a present of a small service to Dr Hurd—'she says the Dr is a very rising man and a thoro' good man—has refus'd being Preceptor to the P. of Wales upon Principles that do him the greatest honour as a Man'. (Hurd must have overcome these scruples, for he accepted the Preceptorship on 5 June 1776. As Turner was appointed Potter to the Prince of Wales in 1784, it is just possible that Hurd, a governor of Brewood Grammar School, who may have known the Turner family in Brewood, recommended him. But more probably the suggestion came from the Marquis of Stafford.)

[9] Hurd's dedication to Sir Edward Littleton, Bart, of his *On Epistolary Writing* (*Works of Richard Hurd*, 1811 edn, i, 10).

[10] Boswell, *Life of Samuel Johnson*, 1824 edn, iv, 403.

[11] G. E. Stringer, *New Hall Porcelain*, 1949, p. 18.

[12] Apprenticeship books at the Public Record Office, London. 'The large village of PENKHULL, which covers the heights above Stoke, appears to have been one of the oldest seats of the earthenware manufacture in this neighbourhood; for we find that as early as 1600 there were here three coarse brown ware potteries, the sites of which have long been occupied by dwelling houses.' (White's *Gazeteer of Staffordshire*, 1834, pp. 534–5.)

[13] W. B. Honey, *English Pottery and Porcelain*, 1962 edn, p. 74.

[14] Shaw, *History of the Staffordshire Potteries* (1829), p. 63.

[15] Shaw, *The Chemistry of Pottery* (1837), p. 416.

[16] Shaw, *History of the Staffordshire Potteries* (1829), p. 157.

[17] The Stoke parish register records the burial of 'Daniel Bird, potter at Stoke', on 10 November 1753. 'His remains', wrote Shaw, 'lie under a dilapidated tomb at the steeple-end of the old church; and the inscription mentions that he was by accident killed at Twickenham, near London' (p. 63). The administration of Bird's goods was granted to his widow, Mary (Somerset House, Admin. of December 1753). A William Bird was buried at Stoke on 23 August 1765. There is a mould in the British Museum inscribed 'William Bird

made me 1751'; and in the Manchester Art Gallery is a dish apparently made with it, decorated in slip. Another entry in the Stoke register records the baptism of Daniel, son of William and Mary Bird, on 27 February 1754. The choice of this Christian name strongly suggests a relationship between William Bird and Daniel Bird the potter. Possibly they were brothers.

A John Bird, an English master potter, was engaged as manager of the Delftfield potteries in Glasgow; in 1748 he sued his employers for wrongful dismissal. (See David Scott-Moncrieff, 'Post-Jacobite Pottery "Boom" ', *The Antique Dealer and Collectors' Guide*, June 1954, pp. 45–46.)

[18] Article in the *Staffordshire Sentinel* of 8 February 1879.

[19] Shaw, *History of the Staffordshire Potteries* (1829), p. 172.

[20] Spode was apprenticed to Whieldon on 9 November 1749. (Arthur Hayden, *Spode and His Successors*, 1925, p. 2.)

[21] 'After [the first] Mr Josiah Spode left the employment of Mr Whieldon, at Fenton, he was employed along with the late Mr Charles Harvey, in the manufactory of Mr Banks [who resided at Stoke Hall] on White Stone Ware, and for Cream Colour, Scratched and Blue Painted.' (Shaw, *History of the Staffordshire Potteries*, 1829, p. 285.)

[22] 'MARRIED. On Monday last, at Trentham, by the Rev. Mr Moss, John Smith Esq., of Great Fenton, one of His Majesty's Justices of the Peace for this county, to Miss E. Turner, of Lane End.' (*Staffordshire Advertiser*, 31 October 1801.)

[23] At p. 12.

[24] *Staffordshire Sentinel*, 8 February 1879.

[25] Shaw, *History of the Staffordshire Potteries* (1829), p. 172.

[26] loc. cit.

[27] See p. 75.

[28] *Proceedings* of the Wedgwood Society, No. 1 (1956), p. 20.

[29] Shaw, *History of the Staffordshire Potteries* (1829), p. 172.

[30] Annie Longton Thomas, *North Staffordshire Transport and Communications in the Eighteenth Century*. (*Collections for a History of Staffordshire*, edited by the William Salt Archaeological Society, 1934, p. 58.)

CHAPTER TWO

Lane End

LANE END LAY at the southern extremity of the Potteries, about four miles south-east of Newcastle-under-Lyme. It was incorporated with Longton in 1848: its inhabitants had found the old name offensive, 'as conveying an idea of meanness which no longer answered to the respectability of the place'.[1] But Lane End did not lose its backwater reputation by changing its name. A writer in *The Leisure Hour* of 2 June 1853 said: 'Longton, or Lane End—if we are to judge from outward demonstrations, [is] the least polished locality in the whole borough.' The anonymous writer of the Introduction to the 1900 edition of Simeon Shaw's *History* said, in a memorable passage which would have to be included in any anthology of English snobbery:

> Longton cleaves unto its own, and its own cleave to it. The special conditions incident to the manufacture of cheap china ware have evolved a type of manufacturer differing considerably from any other, and while it would be a mistake to assume that education and refinement have made less strides in this town than any other in the district, their effects are undoubtedly less in evidence than a certain definite practicalness and directness of speech and action which are more appreciated by the business man than the *litterateur*.

The prejudice is a tenacious one. Today Longton is known—perhaps harking back to the original name—as 'Neck End', and is considered slightly disreputable. 'My mother wouldn't like it if I went with a Neck End girl,' a recent writer on the Potteries was told by his landlady's son.[2]

By 1848 Lane End was a prosperous potting town, but in 1762, according to Ward, there were only 1,300 inhabitants in Longton and Lane End together.[3] When Wesley passed through in 1784 it was still small enough to be called a village.[4] Eight years later the district was visited by the Hon. John Byng, author of the *Torrington Diaries*, who wrote:

> At Lane End, the population of the pottery commences (where the roads are repaired by fragments 'broke in pieces, like a potter's vessel') and continues a street of many miles;—the men, whiten'd with the powder, are supplied with coals, to keep alive the

everlasting ovens, from every adjacent field; hundreds of horses and asses with paniers, are incessantly taking in their lading: thro' there I pass'd along, slowly in pleasant rumination; but wonder'd much at no market being establish'd for such a multitude.[5]

By 1818 the population of Longton and Lane End had swollen to 4,930.[6] Shaw in 1819 observed that Lane End had been for many years notable for the great irregularity in the position of its buildings, ranging from the respectable residence of the manufacturer to the mud and saggar hovel of the pauper, and scattered over a wide area: 'but in comparatively recent times, under the almost magic influence of a prosperous manufacture, improvement has commenced'.[7]

As elsewhere, physical improvement did not necessarily bring with it mental enlightenment. The old savage sports persisted in the Potteries—bull-baiting, cock- and dog-fighting. Indeed, the Industrial Revolution helped to perpetuate them: the energies frustrated in tedious factory jobs found their outlet in the frenzy of brutal spectacle. One of Turner's most successful designs shows a cock-fight. The Spode-Copeland factory museum possesses the master mould of the audience in the pit (Plate 17a), and Mr E. N. Stretton owns a caneware jug (Plate 17b) showing the full scene. In 1869 a 'Commissioner' of the magazine *Good Words* visited Staffordshire, to provide material for a series called *Toiling and Moiling: Some Account of our Working People, and How They Live*. He wrote with sympathy, though also with some of the condescension implied by his title. The article recorded some recollections of the 1819–29 period by an old potter:

> Next day I foregathered with a potter of the old school. . . . A remark on the unexpected quietness of the Potteries unlocks the old man's memories. 'Th'wouldn'st ha' thowt so fifty yare back, nor forty nayther. Theer wor cockin' an' dog foitin' then. . . . Ah moind, when ah wor a lahd, mah feyther an' another chep backed a cock agin a parson's for ten poond a soide. Mah feyther wor a teelor, an' t'other chep wor a waver. Yer've heered about t'old witch o' Lane End? Doan't metter—she wor well knawed in these parts; an' mah feyther took a feather o' his cock to t'old witch an' she charmed un; an' as soon as the cocks wor put down, parson's turns ower, an' wouldn't so mooch as look at t'other. "You've been to t'devil," says parson; "boot ah've got a stronger devil than yourn"; an' he broke t'charm, an' his cock won arter hall.'[8]

From all this oblique evidence, we may assume that the Lane End to which John Turner and his wife came in 1759 was a ramshackle hamlet with a small and superstitious population, the master potters living in comfortable houses, the workers in cottages or shacks. According to Henry Wedgwood, the Turners lived in Chancery Lane, Longton, but circumstantial evidence suggests that they may

also have lived at some time in Meir House, a Georgian building which was demolished shortly before the last war, about the same time as the destruction of the
original Longton Hall. Mrs Eric Young has given to the Hanley Reference Library
two volumes of the *Staffordshire Advertiser* which she inherited with the family
collection of pottery. These, covering the periods January 1795–December 1799
and January 1800–December 1804, are both inscribed:

> John Turner Lane End 1835.
> The gift of his uncle, Martin John Wright.

Martin John Wright was the brother of Elizabeth Wright of Stafford who
married William Turner in 1799; the John Turner to whom the volumes were
presented was William Turner's son, who became a chemist at Lane End; 1835
was the year of William Turner's death.

John Turner the chemist made an index, in the front and back of the volumes,
to all the passages relating to the Turner family. Thus he records: 'November
26 1803 Uncle John Turner married.' (John Turner II married Mary Hyde of
Manchester on that date.) And again: 'Aunt Smith married 31 October 1801.'
(Elizabeth, daughter of John Turner I, married John Smith of Great Fenton on
that date.)

One of these pencilled entries reads: 'School at Meir House, Jan 7 1797.'

The passage thus indexed is an advertisement:

> Meir House, near Lane End
> STAFFORDSHIRE.
> Mrs TURNER

Respectfully informs her Friends and the Public, that her School will open after the
Christmas Recess, on the 21st inst.

TERMS

	£	s	d
Board, Needle Work, and Grammar Per Annum	14	14	0
Entrance	1	1	0
Music, Per Quarter	1	1	0
Entrance	1	1	0
Dancing, Per Quarter	0	15	0
Entrance	0	10	6
Drawing, Per Quarter	0	15	0
Entrance	0	10	6
Writing, Per Quarter	0	7	6
Entrance	0	5	0

	£	s	d
Washing, Per Quarter	0	10	6
Day Scholars, Per Quarter	0	12	0
Entrance	0	10	6

Each Lady is required to bring one pair of Sheets, Three Towels, Knife Fork and Silver Spoon, the spoon to be returned.—As Mrs T. takes a limited number, a Quarter's Notice is expected before any Lady leaves the School. Meir House is a short distance from Lane End, and a healthy eligible situation.

Who was the Mrs Turner referred to? She could not have been John Turner I's wife, who died, according to her Brewood tombstone, in 1777. Nor could she be the wife of either William or John II, as they did not marry until 1799 and 1803 respectively. I have been unable to discover her identity, but the fact that the passage is indexed makes it almost certain that she was a part of our Turner family. David Lea Turner of Southampton, the oldest surviving male descendant of John Turner I, recalled *Weir* House as the name of the family property. Since weir is a word in common use, and meir is not,[9] the tradition might easily have become distorted in this way in a branch of the family which early emancipated itself from the *patria potestas* in Staffordshire.

In 1762 John Turner's first son, William, was born; 1762 is also the year of the first dated example of Turner pottery. In the *Connoisseur* of May 1907 there appeared an article entitled 'A Notable Turner Teapot'. At that time, it belonged to Mr A. E. Chavasse, of the Avenue, Stone, Staffordshire, but its present whereabouts is unknown, and Chavasse did not leave a will. The teapot, impressed TURNER, was 5 in high, with a buff-coloured earthenware body. An elaborate design in relief showed 'a young man in middle eighteenth-century costume, dangling from his right hand one male doll, and from his left, two female dolls, dressed in costume of the same period'. Beneath the figure, and running round the teapot was the inscription:

LORD TRENTHAM WITH HIS FRENCH DOLLS

The design was completed by conventional flowers and foliage, the whole outlined in a rich dark blue. On the base was the underglaze inscription:

M. Degg. Mar., 1762

and inside the lid, the inscription:

M.D. Uttoxeter.

The Deggs were one of the best-known Uttoxeter families. Sir Simon Degg (1612–

1704) was author of *The Parson's Counsellor*, and Dr Plot refers to him as 'the learned and ingenious Sir Simon Degg Knight'. The Staffordshire historian William Pitt records that the last male member of the Degg family, a pauper, was buried in Uttoxeter in about 1812.[10]

The inscription on the teapot is interesting as an early use of the word 'doll', which first appeared in print in the *Gentleman's Magazine* of 1751.[11] In this context the word probably refers to a French toy, the *pantin*, which took the town by storm from 1748 to 1756, a pasteboard puppet so strung together that by every touch of the finger it was thrown into grotesque antics. The *Connoisseur* wondered why the 'young man'—Lord Trentham—should be portrayed holding French dolls, and hinted at some obscure local scandal or political lampoon. But in 1762 Lord Trentham was four years old: the teapot evidently shows nothing more than a child with his toys. The Marquis of Stafford, Lord Trentham's father, was the leviathan of Staffordshire. In addition to his Trentham demesne, he owned large estates at Stittenham in Yorkshire and Lilleshall in Shropshire. The heir to these fortunes, and the patronage they carried, would attract the same popular interest in Staffordshire as the heir to the throne in London. In the absence of a local Press, the potters satisfied the public curiosity, in this as in other matters: the Willett Collection in the Brighton Art Gallery was formed entirely from pieces illustrating contemporary people and events, the ceramic equivalents of broadsheets.

Lord Trentham's father was a notorious devotee of French fashions. To the disgust of John Byng,[12] he filled Trentham House with French furniture. It was therefore natural that he should buy marionettes for his son. Thirty years later, as Earl Gower, Lord Trentham was ambassador to France in the Revolution—the consummation, and presumably the end, of the family Francophilia. It was he who saved William Turner from the guillotine.

NOTES TO CHAPTER TWO

[1] J. Ward, *The Borough of Stoke-upon-Trent* (1843), p. 555.
[2] Mervyn Jones, *Potbank* (1961), p. 89.
[3] John Ward, *The Borough of Stoke-upon-Trent* (1843), p. 43.
[4] John Wesley, *Journal*, 29 March 1784.
[5] John Byng, *A Tour of the North*, 28 June 1792.

[6] W. Parson and T. Bradshaw, *Staffordshire General and Commercial Directory for 1818*, part I. There were 2,277 males and 2,653 females—1,079 families in all, inhabiting 1,032 houses.

[7] Simeon Shaw, *History of the Staffordshire Potteries* (1829), pp. 72–73.

[8] *Good Words*, 1 March 1869. It is interesting to note that in the last conviction for cock-fighting in England two of the defendants were resident in Stoke-on-Trent (*The Times*, 15 September 1956). In the last previous conviction two of the defendants lived at Trentham (*The Times*, 17 July 1928).

[9] In Staffordshire, a 'meir' or mere is a pit from which clay has been excavated, and which has later filled with water. There is still a district of Longton named Meir; the original name of Lane End was Meare Lane End (*Victoria History of Staffordshire*, viii, 226).

[10] William Pitt, *Topographical History of Staffordshire* (1817), p. 207.

[11] See Leslie Daiken, *Children's Toys Throughout the Ages* (1953), p. 102.

[12] *The Torrington Diaries*, ed. by C. Bruyn Andrews, 1934–8, iii, 156–7.

CHAPTER THREE

The Wares

AT LANE END, Shaw tells us, John Turner 'manufactured every kind of Pottery then in demand, and also introduced some other kinds not previously known'.[1] The Degg teapot, the 'agate' jug in the Schreiber Collection, and probably also the salt-glaze wares in Mrs Young's possession, are examples of Turner's work in traditional materials.

Black basalt, although an obvious vehicle for the lapidary expressions of neo-classicism, had been known to the Staffordshire potters as 'Egyptian Black' for more than half a century before Wedgwood adopted it as a staple. Shaw in one book ascribes its origin to the Elers brothers,[2] and in another book to Wood of Hot Lane in 1700.[3] Wedgwood's first experiments with Egyptian Black were made in the seventeen-sixties. Turner's first basalt pieces probably date from the next decade.

The Turners' black basalt wares are among the least common of their productions, and must amount to only a tithe of those produced by Wedgwood. Artistically they represent the extreme limits of the Turners' achievement in the neo-classical style. Colonel Grant, author of *The Makers of Black Basaltes* (1910), had in his collection two teapots of great elegance and formal simplicity (Grant, Plate LXIII). Like the equally successful fluted sugar-boxes (Grant, Plate LXI, Fig. 2), they were modelled on silver originals. But compare these with the grotesque tripod lamp (Grant, Plate LX, Fig. 2) or the bloated jug with the lumpish freize of oak leaves and acorns (Grant, Plate LXI, Fig. 1). In these graceless pieces we see the nadir of neo-classicism. In our own illustrations the debasement of style can be judged by a comparison of the silver-pattern teapot (Plate 9a) with the coffee-pot (Plate 9b). The teapot has the same qualities as those illustrated by Grant: a unity and strength of composition, an austere elegance reminiscent of the work of the silversmith Hester Bateman. The coffee-pot shows a displeasing coalition of contrary ornament: Greek fret, broad and narrow fluting, Widow of Zarapeth, acanthus leaves. These severe motifs, architectural, Biblical and botanical, are thrown together on a vessel sinuous and somewhat flamboyant in shape.

The difference in style illustrates a difference in period. Almost certainly the teapot was made by the elder Turner, the coffee-pot by his sons. The artistic decline was accompanied by a degeneration in technique, of which Colonel Grant's description could scarcely be bettered:

> There is a slight, but very distinct difference discernable between the Basaltes manufactured by Turner *père* and that manufactured by his sons. The ware of the former is usually to be distinguished from Wedgwood's by a faint greyish or silvery tinge, and a just perceptible increase of stoniness to the touch; it is usually thinner, also, and shows less latheing on the insides and bottoms of vessels. These parts are often quite rough, in marked contradistinction to the exquisite finish of the exteriors.
>
> Turner's sons, while preserving every other characteristic, seem to have added an ingredient to the formula which bestowed upon their paste a faint, very faint, greenish hue. This is too frequent to be a mere accident of firing, and it seems to occur in the most highly finished pieces. There is, too, a certain facility, what painters term 'slickness', about their mouldings and reliefs, not noticeable in the elder potter's work. It is as if the various designs had by that time become items of an extensive routine, entailing a certain loss of individuality in their modelling and application.[4]

In some respects John Turner's basalt ware was superior to that of Wedgwood. Of the sugar-boxes already mentioned Grant writes:

> The outer sugar-boxes well illustrate his mastery in . . . fine-fluting. In this particular, Turner surpassed Wedgwood, who, as has been said, did not often employ the device. The Lane End potter managed to give to the ridge and furrow of the work a roundness and softness beside which Wedgwood's fluting appears somewhat harsh and mechanical. The former, too, was wont to pack into an inch of surface a greater number of striations than any of his brethren. I have counted on a cream jug no fewer than thirty-four rounds and hollows in an inch of surface, the multitudinous flutes being beautifully graduated so as to fade into all but invisibility as they approach the foot of the piece. On the lids of these two sugar-boxes the flutings actually disappear, as imperceptibly as streamlets running into sand, into the blank which surrounds the knob.[5]

Turner invented his jasper ware, as he invented his black basalt, quite independently of Wedgwood.[6] The early Turner jasper wares have in their composition no trace of barytes, the distinguishing ingredient of Wedgwood's formula.[7] Some of the pieces produced after 1790, however, were of true jasper composition. Turner's own jasper is generally of a more slaty blue than the most familiar Wedgwood variation, and has a more vitreous appearance. It is rarely of the harsh deep blue favoured by William Adams. In the TURNER & CO. period a brilliant peacock blue became the most common ground.

In their jasper wares the Turners are at their least original. Most of their classical reliefs were copied from Wedgwood designs. The insipid material gave little scope for the satirical English scenes in which the Turner modellers excelled. It required demure Arcadian vignettes, and Wedgwood rightly appraised the medium when he commissioned designs from Lady Templetown, Lady Diana Beauclerk, and the passionless, academical Flaxman. Stubbs's 'Frightened Horse' design, it is true, showed what could be done in a less rarified genre, but the public did not appreciate melodrama at the tea-table: a tea-cup was not the place for an epic.

At its best—for example, the scent-bottle (Plate 3a), and the later tea set (Plate 6)—Turner jasper rivals Wedgwood's in workmanship, though to my knowledge the Turners never attempted the coloured jaspers of Wedgwood, the pink, lilac, yellow and sage green. It is hard to decide whether this is evidence of superior taste or of inferior technique.

We know from John Turner's will that he was an experimentalist.[8] William Burton, writing in 1904, recorded 'an old tradition in the potteries that John Turner sacrificed many an ovenful of ware to secure the success of his trials and experiments'.[9] Henry Wedgwood tells us that he was dedicated to his trade, and spent days trudging over the Staffordshire countryside with a horse laden with panniers, to bring back samples of clay.[10] In 1775 he and Josiah Wedgwood went clay-hunting together in Cornwall. But as it happened Turner found what he was looking for on his own doorstep.

> About 1780 [wrote Shaw] he discovered a vein of fine Clay, on the land at Green Dock, now the property of Mr Ephraim Hobson, of Hanley. From this he obtained all his supplies for manufacturing his beautiful and excellent Stone Ware Pottery, of a cane colour; which he formed into very beautiful Jugs, with ornamental designs, and the most tasteful articles of domestic use. Some of them are excellent Wine Coolers; others represent different kinds of Pastry, as Tureens, Butter Coolers, &c. and are well calculated to deceive the eye at a short distance. An instance of this deception occurred to the author, being seated in the parlour, where there was a Lady's work-basket, which he was led to consider from its appearance as *twig* or willow ware, and was most agreeably surprised, to find it of cane coloured pottery. The deception was not single; for a young Lady, on a visit, had made a similar mistake on the day preceding.[11]

What John Turner had discovered was a fine peacock marl, from which a variety of stonewares could be produced, ranging in colour from a mealy white to a rich sunny ochre. The new clay engendered a style appropriate to it. Though capable of great technical refinement, it was essentially a rustic material. It demanded something more humane than the frigid bas-reliefs of neo-classicism.

Turner's modellers designed a series of English rural scenes, hit off with a satirical verve in the tradition of Hogarth and Rowlandson. Even Professor Church, who saw in Wedgwood the destroyer of the Englishness of English ceramics, was seduced by these designs into a reluctant admiration for the so-called imitator of Wedgwood.[12]

At the Spode-Copeland factory museum the sprig-moulds of the designs used on Turner's fine stoneware are conveniently assembled in trays. The English subjects are:

Cock fighting (after Hogarth)
The kill
Britannia supported by two soldiers, a private of the line and a cavalryman
Britannia succouring a slave
A Gretna Green marriage
Falstaff in the linen basket (*The Merry Wives of Windsor*)
Uncle Toby
A toper
Smokers round a pembroke table
Village musicians
A potter at the wheel
The archery lesson

The last-named design is at once the most successful and most common of all the reliefs. It occurs on a mug mounted in silver with the London date-mark for 1794 (Plate 15). The fashion for toxophily was set by the first Marchioness of Salisbury in garden parties at Hatfield from 1789 onwards. A print entitled 'Archery at Hatfield' (Corbold del. Cook sculpt.), published on 1 December 1792 by J. Wheble of Warwick Lane, London, shows women archers in costume identical to that on the 1794 mug, and indeed may have been the original from which the Turner design was adapted. Mr. Reginald Haggar, in his *English Country Pottery* (1950), Plate 14B, illustrates an 'archery lesson' jug by Felix Pratt of Fenton, the figures being painted in characteristic Pratt colours.

When I visited the Spode-Copeland factory in 1963 I was delighted to see a jug being made with Turner's 'Uncle Toby' relief as the principal decoration. The art director of the firm, Mr Harold Holdway, also showed me four white parian plaques which the factory was producing from Turner moulds (Uncle Toby, the toper, the Gretna Green marriage, and the potter at the wheel). These plaques, which are impressed TURNER on the front, bear the Spode mark on the back to avoid any possibility of deception. Framed in black velvet, they were being sold by two London stores.

The 'pastry ware' to which Shaw refers was not intended, as his account would suggest, merely as a kind of ceramic joke. It was made at a time when flour was in short supply. Captain Jeffs, in *The Life of George Brummell, Esq.* (1844), wrote that

> the scarcity two years after Brummell's retirement (viz. in July 1800) was so great that the consumption of flour for pastry was prohibited in the Royal Household, rice being used instead; the distiller left off malting; hackney-coach fares were raised twenty-five per cent. and Wedgwood made dishes to represent pie-crust.[13]

At Lane End there were bread riots. One of the passages indexed in the Turner copies of the *Staffordshire Advertiser* is the following, of 3 May 1800:

RIOTS

We are extremely concerned to state, that an alarming spirit of disorder has manifested itself in several parts of this country.—On Monday a mob assembled at Lane End, in the Pottery, and seized a quantitity of potatoes, flour, & etc. which they disposed of among themselves. The riot becoming very serious and alarming, the Volunteers were called out, through whose exertions the ringleaders were secured, and seven of them were brought to our prison, guarded by a party of the Newcastle and Pottery troop of Cavalry.

Doubtless Major William Turner, of the Volunteers, helped to put down these riots.

An example of the Turners' pastry ware is shown in Plate 21b; an identical piece, also marked TURNER, is in the Buten Museum of Wedgwood, Merion, Pennsylvania. William Burton wrote:

> A tradition has been handed down in Longton that, as a *tour-de-force* of imitative skill, he made in pottery a group of vessels shaped and coloured like the actual roasts of one of the homely country feasts of the day. A baron of beef, a roast leg of mutton, a sucking pig, goose, turkey, and many other pieces completed this queer assemblage, which on completion was exhibited at one of the inns of Lane End, where it made a nine-days' wonder for the countryside. In the Mayer Collection at Liverpool are four or five such pieces with Turner's name impressed in them, and, whilst we may smile at the rustic taste of such productions, we must admit that they are triumphs of technical skill.[14]

Unfortunately, the Liverpool Museum was bombed during the last war, and although restoration work is in progress, the Mayer Collection has not yet been re-opened to the public.

Turner's white stoneware and caneware tended to take the place, in his productions, of the creamware and pearlware from which Wedgwood and most of his contemporaries made their domestic wares. But the Turners did also make cream

and pearl colour, especially for their foreign markets. In Delft, John Turner had a
decorating establishment, where Dutch enamellers painted his plates, chiefly with
Biblical scenes. Plate 33b shows such a plate, made for sale to pilgrims visiting the
shrine at Kevelaar. Another series was decorated with scenes from the story of the
Prodigal Son, the figures dressed with charming anachronism in eighteenth-
century costume. A characteristic of this Dutch decoration is an ornate *scraffito*
work: elaborate arabesques are scratched in the surface of the paint, as, for example, in the father's coat and mother's gown of Plate 33a. The most common
colours were a rich sorrel red, a watery green and a deep mazarine blue.

Turner's ware had a great sale in Holland, because of its strength and ability
to resist high temperatures. It was introduced by his agents, Sanderson (an Englishman) and Bellaert,[15] and was imitated by Arend de Haak.[16] As early as 1765
MacPherson, in the *Annals of Commerce*, could write that:

> Formerly, we ate all our meat off plates made at Delf in Holland; now the Dutch
> generally use our Staffordshire plates.[17]

And on 16 September 1895 M. de Laigue, the French Consul in Rotterdam,
recalled in a letter to the Minister of Foreign Affairs, that:

> A la fin du XVIIIᵉ siècle, l'industrie céramique de Delft fut ruinée par l'importation
> des faïences anglaises.[18]

Some of Turner's creamware, which, with its primrose-yellow glaze, has more
in common with Leeds pottery[19] than Wedgwood's cream colour, was decorated
in England. Mr Donald Towner has in his collection a narrow mug painted with
the slogan 'Rodney for Ever' which he ascribes to Turner.

In 1779 Wedgwood invented his 'pearlware',[20] so named because of the
nacreous effect produced by a bluish glaze on a very white body. Although less
pleasant in appearance than creamware, it was stronger and more heat-resistant.
The two drug-jars (Plate 32a) are of pearlware; so are the plate and teapot (Plates
28b and c), decorated by, or in the manner of, 'the painter of the tulip with divergent petals'.[21] The Turners continued to make pearlware in the early nineteenth
century. An example is the plate decorated with reversible heads (Plate 38), one
of a series which included, besides Grandmama/Miss, Doctor/Divine, Thomas/
Sally and Groaner/Grinner. The reversible head, a kind of pictorial palindrome,
has been a recurring convention of English humour from Hogarth to *OHO* by
Rex and Laurence Whistler. In ceramics, and especially in domestic wares, where
some degree of symmetry is inevitable, it is a particularly effective device, since it
can be modelled as well as painted or printed on the surface. The Schreiber Col-

lection contains two mugs moulded with Pope/Devil heads. The contrast between
courtship and marriage was a favourite, and Mr Reginald Haggar describes a mug
transfer-printed with this motif, with appropriate doggerel beneath:

> When two fond fools together meet
> Each look gives joy each kiss so sweet;
> But wed, how cold and cross they'll be,
> Turn upside down and then you'll see.[22]

From the lack of accomplishment of the creamware and pearlware examples
extant, it is evident that Turner did not think these materials fit for aristocratic
tables, unlike Wedgwood, who made creamware services for Queen Charlotte and
Catherine the Great of Russia.

Like their father, the brothers Turner made important innovations in potting
technique. 'Mr (William) Turner', wrote Shaw, 'succeeded in making a Shining
Blue glazed Pottery, similar to that of the Japanese Porcelain; an imitation of which
had been attempted by Mr Cookworthy; and was pronounced by Mr Wedgwood,
as a *desideratum.*'[23] I have seen a number of examples of 'Shining Blue' pottery,
dating from the first decades of the nineteenth century, and some with familiar
Turner reliefs in white. But none of these pieces is marked. Some of them are
certainly not by the Turners, judging by the reliefs; these may perhaps be attributed to Spode.

More important was the invention, by William Turner, of a new kind of
stoneware.

In 1800 [wrote Shaw] Mr W. Turner having amused himself with examining by
chemical analysis the different strata perforated in sinking a new shaft of a Coal Pit
at Milfield Gate, discovered, in what is called the Tabberner's (or Little) Mine, a
mineral, which by calcination becomes a pearl white, yet unlike other minerals, does
not *shrink* by the most ardent temperature to which it has been subjected—130 of
Wedgwood's pyrometer. This is now called *Patent Stone*, in consequence of the
brothers Turner having obtained Letters Patent for manufacturing with it as one
material, a real Porcelain, wholly different from any previously manufactured. The
stone is very different from the *Iron Stone*; and therefore the present Patent Ironstone
China must not be confounded with the other Patent Porcelains, Champion's and
Turners'. The late J. Spode, Esq. purchased the right to manufacture this patent
Stone Porcelain; and a fine specimen of it has already been noticed. . . .

Early in the present century, Capt. Winter having boasted that the Articles of his
manufacture, at Tunstall were the only *true Porcelain* made in Staffordshire, experienced no little chagrin, on ascertaining that his ware would fuse at a heat much
below that usually required to fire Mr Turner's, and that while his *contracted* in the

same manner as other productions of the district, Mr Turner's retained its size un-
affected in shape or expansion; at which fact, Dr Hope, of Edinburgh, expressed his
surprize, in language most complimentary. But, at the time when most benefit might
have accrued to Mr Turner, in consequence of the celebrity which his Porcelain had
acquired, the late Mr Harwood, of Newcastle, Steward of the late Marquis of Stafford,
interdicted any further supplies of the stone indispensibly requisite, under the
pretext that the Marquis was offended at the Patent having been obtained, and would
not encourage any *monopoly*!

Singular, indeed, that the manufacture of Porcelain under one Patent, should be
prevented in such an authoritative and aristocratic manner, (tho' probably the
ostensible denouncer was wholly ignorant of the procedure of his agent,) while another
person secured great advantages. But the Marquis might have been excited to this
procedure, by a remembrance of the opposition Messrs Turner's father had manifested
towards the extension of the Patent Term to Mr Champion.[24]

The Turners' patent, No. 2367, was taken out on 19 January 1800. The
specification describes the process in detail. The new stone, known as 'The
Tabberner's Mine Rock', 'Little Mine Rock', and 'New Rock', was reduced to a
fine powder by grinding it in a potter's mill in the same way as flints were usually
ground, but without calcination. The powder was dried in a kiln, mixed with an
equal proportion of growan, or Cornish stone, then with water, and passed through
a fine lawn sieve. It was then ready for moulding into vessels. The advantages of
the new method were, first, that because of its great ductility larger pieces of ware
could be formed than before (one of the Turners' modellers made a 22-gallon punchbowl from it);[25] secondly, that it was less liable to accidents in the kiln than other
stonewares, because of the moderate degree of heat required to fire it (it could be
burnt in the same kiln as creamware); finally, since the raw material was found in
coal-mines, which had to be excavated in any case, great expense was saved.

In appearance the new stoneware (marked Turner's Patent in red enamel) is
similar to Mason's Ironstone China. The most common design was that shown in
Plates 36 and 37. If the Marquis of Stafford had not prevented the Turners from
obtaining supplies of the stone, the new stoneware might have enabled them to
recoup their fortunes. As it was, other potters benefited from William Turner's
discovery.

NOTES TO CHAPTER THREE

[1] Simeon Shaw, *History of the Staffordshire Potteries* (1829), p. 172.

[2] ibid., p. 118.

[3] Simeon Shaw, *The Chemistry of Pottery* (1837), p. 416.

[4] M. H. Grant, *The Makers of Black Basaltes* (1910), p. 209.

[5] ibid., pp. 217–18.

[6] Wedgwood himself wrote of his jasper that 'The first nearly similar effect was produced by an intelligent neighbour, with a material different from that employed by Mr Wedgwood'. Jewitt, who quotes this passage (*Life of Josiah Wedgwood*, 1865, p. 321), adds in a footnote that the 'neighbour' was Turner.

[7] On p. 157 of his *History and Description of English Earthenware and Stoneware* (1904), William Burton, F.C.S., published his analysis of Turner's so-called 'jasper'. The breakdown was as follows:

SiO	53.95	MgO	0.76
AlO	34.00	NaO	0.37
CaO	7.53	KO	3.41

[8] 'I do hereby further direct that my said sons shall become equally intitled to the benefit of all experiments made by me in the course of my Trade or Business as a Potter and to all secrets in my possession relating to the Manufactury of Porcelain or Earthenware.'

[9] William Burton, *A History and Description of English Earthenware and Stoneware* (1904), p. 154n.

[10] *Staffordshire Sentinel*, 8 February 1879.

[11] Simeon Shaw, *History of the Staffordshire Potteries* (1829), pp. 172–3.

[12] 'Turner was not a mere plagiarist of Wedgwood, many of his productions having marked elements of originality.' (Arthur H. Church, *English Earthenware*, 1911, p. 115.)

[13] Quoted, *Catalogue of Specimens in the Museum of Practical Geology* (1876), p. 131.

[14] William Burton, *A History and Description of English Earthenware and Stoneware* (1904), p. 156.

[15] W. P. Knowles, *Dutch Pottery and Porcelain* (1904), p. 111.

[16] ibid., p. 110.

[17] David MacPherson, *Annals of Commerce* (1805 edn), iii, 430.

[18] Quoted by Henry-Pierre Fourest, *Les Faïences de Delft* (1957), p. 17.

[19] Donald Towner, *English Cream-Coloured Earthenware* (1957), p. 17.

[20] See *Wedgwood Dates and Marks, 1730–1820*, a chart compiled and issued by the Wedgwood Society, 1959.

[21] See p. 30 of the present work.

[22] R. G. Haggar, *English Country Pottery* (1950), p. 63.

[23] Simeon Shaw, *History of the Staffordshire Potteries* (1829), p. 222.

[24] ibid., pp. 229–30. For an account of John Turner I's opposition to Richard Champion, see Chapter V of the present work.

[25] The modeller was William Massey. See pp. 24–5 of the present work.

CHAPTER FOUR

Modellers and Decorators

IN SPITE OF Wedgwood's policy of suppressing his modellers' identities,[1] we know in many cases the names of the men and women who designed particular bas-reliefs: William Hackwood, John Flaxman, Lady Templetown, and others. Owing to the scarcity of documents, it is not possible to identify many Turner productions as the work of any one artist. But the sources tell us something of the men. 'Their principal modeller', writes Shaw, 'was Mr Jas Luckock, a person of great skill, and most extensive acquirements as an Artist.'[2] Nothing further is known of Luckock, though possibly he was related to that John Lucock who manufactured porcelain at Liverpool with Thomas Wolfe and Miles Mason (both Staffordshire potters) from 1796 to 1800.

There are a number of references to William Massey, another modeller who worked for the Turners. The earliest mention of him is by Shaw:

> Mr Fletcher, of Edinburgh, of Sporting celebrity, having given an order to a tradesman at Edinburgh, for a very large Punch Bowl, the order had been forwarded to different celebrated Potters, and remained not executed. Application was ultimately made to Mr Turner, whose throwers attempted by different processes to accomplish the object; but it was only fully and satisfactorily got into form, by the ingenuity of Mr William Massey, the Modeller, now resident at Stoke. It holds *twenty-two* Gallons Imperial Measure; and is now preserved in the Museum at Edinburgh. On its outside is a kind of tablet, on which are beautifully enamelled, a Chinese Town, and the Names of the Persons and Place, as well as the date. The late John Daniel, Esq. mentioned this specimen in terms of the most glowing description.[3]

The 'Edinburgh Museum' must refer to the collection of the Society of Antiquaries of Scotland (now the National Museum of Antiquities of Scotland), an eighteenth-century foundation; the Royal Scottish Museum was not founded until 1854, when it absorbed the relevant university collections, and all the Edinburgh Corporation museums are of comparatively recent foundation. But there is no record of the Massey punchbowl at any of these places.[4] Presumably it was broken, lost, or withdrawn by the original lender.

In Mr Geoffrey Godden's collection there is a self-portrait of Massey (Plate 19a), well modelled in a highly vitreous caneware. The following inscription was incised into the back before firing:

14 Oct. 1835 Wm Masey alias Poor Pilgarlic.[5] This portrait of himself was executed by the author in the 60th year of his practice as a Modeller and presented to E. Jones.

A comparison of the self-portrait plaque with a figure group of the Parson and Clerk (Plate 19b) strongly suggests that Massey may have modelled the latter also. The group, marked TURNER, is of the same glittering stoneware as the plaque; the details of buttons, hair, and eyes are extremely similar to those of the portrait. The original from which the Parson and Clerk group was copied was probably designed by one of the Wood family, who also produced the anti-sacerdotal 'Vicar and Moses'. The Parson and Clerk group was imitated by a number of potters, including William Adams.[6]

Massey's death certificate at Somerset House shows that he died at Stoke-on-Trent on 17 March 1839, aged 69. He was born, then, in 1770, and therefore, if his own account is to be believed, began work at the age of 5. Chaffers wrote: 'The William Massey here mentioned was born in 1770, he was the seventh son of the seventh son, in the twenty-seventh year of his mother's life; in 1834 he was the survivor of seventeen children, and the father of seven children, and altogether an eccentric.'[7] In 1834 Massey was living at Market Street, Stoke-on-Trent.[8] His obituary said:

DIED. At Stoke-upon-Trent, on the 17th instant, Mr William Massey, modeller, aged 69. He was an original genius, and many works of great beauty now extant in the Potteries, were executed by him. In the infancy of potting he contributed in a considerable degree by his well-known talents to the advancement of this beautiful portion of our national industry.[9]

Like Massey, George Ray, another Turner modeller, is known to us as the author of one documentary work, again a stoneware portrait—the bust illustrated in Plate 39. It was bought by the Hanley Museum in 1936 for the extraordinary sum of £2. 12s. 6d. It is inscribed on the back: 'G. Ray. Modeler [*sic*] Lane End.' The subject of the bust has been variously identified as John Turner I, William Turner, and John Turner II. It is illustrated in *Staffordshire Pottery* by Josiah Wedgwood, M.P. (later Lord Wedgwood of Barlaston), and Thomas H. Ormsbee (1947). The caption reads:

William Turner. This pottery bust, attributed to Hackwood, was made circa 1780. It portrays William Turner, master potter of Lane End. He made basalt pieces of high quality. He was the brother of John and son of John Turner who died in 1786. The two brothers carried on the family pottery at Lane End until 1803.[10]

It would scarcely be possible to concentrate more errors in as many words. In the first place, Hackwood modelled for Wedgwood, not Turner; and in any case the bust is signed 'G. Ray'. Secondly, in 1780, the date to which Wedgwood and Ormsbee assign the bust, William Turner, the suggested sitter, was 18 years old: the bust shows an elderly man in costume of the 1830s. John Turner I died in 1787, not 1786. Finally, John Turner II withdrew from the partnership in 1804, and production continued until 1829.

But William Turner's candidature has a more doughty champion—Mr Reginald Haggar, who in his *Staffordshire Chimney Ornaments* writes:

> There is a fine cane stoneware bust of him (William Turner) in Hanley Museum, inscribed 'G. Ray modeller Lane End', which is full of individuality and character.[11]

Mr. Haggar further discovered that George Ray was living at Liverpool Road, Stoke, in 1834; and at 8 Normacot Road, Longton, from 1860 to 1864.[12]

The disappearance of Ray's name from the local directories after 1864 suggested that he might have died in that or the following year. A search at Somerset House revealed that George Ray, modeller, died in New Street, Longton, on 6 May 1865, aged 54 years. He was born, therefore, in 1811.

This discovery puts paid to Mr G. E. Stringer's suggestion, in *New Hall Porcelain*, that 'In my opinion the bust which Wedgwood (i.e. Lord Wedgwood) has reproduced is that of "the elder Mr Turner", the probable associate of Richard Champion and the probable promoter of the New Hall Company.'[13] John Turner I died in 1787; Ray was born more than twenty years later. Mr Stringer's attribution was wishful thinking: he wanted the bust to be of John Turner I, and not one of the sons, who, unlike their father, had no connexion with the New Hall factory.

The earliest mention of the Ray bust occurs in William Burton's *History and Description of English Earthenware and Stoneware* (1904):

> The most interesting of these busts known to the author is one, nearly life-size, of the second John Turner, which is in the possession of Mr Bernard Moore, of Longton; it is inscribed at the back 'E. Ray, Modeller, Longton'.[14]

The inaccuracies in the transcription—the wrong initial and the substitution of 'Longton' for 'Lane End'—warn us to be chary of accepting Burton's attribution. But in any case John Turner II died in 1824, and even if the bust had been modelled in that year Ray would have been only 13 years old, while the bust is evidently the work of a mature and experienced modeller.

In fact, then, William is the only one of the Turners who can possibly be represented by the bust. For he did not die until 1835, by which date Ray would be 24. The costume of the sitter suggests a date between 1830 and 1840. He is evidently an old man. William Turner was 68 in 1830, and 73 when he died. There is no absolute proof that the bust portrays any of the Turners. But that it does has at least never been questioned, and William Turner is named as the subject in the Hanley Museum catalogue.

William Greatbatch[15] was both a modeller and a decorator. His name is linked with the Turner factory in a letter written by Wedgwood's nephew, Thomas Byerley, to Josiah Wedgwood II:

> William Greatbatch came to Etruria in 1788—when Thomas Wedgwood declared his intention of settling at Hill House with his family—W.G. & all his family were at the time in Turner's employ—who on the old man going away sent all the rest after him—and all came to Etruria.[16]

A passage in Simeon Shaw suggests one way in which Greatbatch and Turner might have become acquainted:

> The father of William Greatbatch, was a farmer, at Berryhill; and supplied coals to the manufacturers at Fenton, from Botteslow and Colamoor; and among others, to Mr Whieldon, and Mr Daniel Bird, on the backs of horses, the roads being then so bad that had a horse stumbled, or missed his step into the holes, he certainly would have fallen, and with difficulty would have been again raised.[17]

So Greatbatch's father not only had dealings with Thomas Whieldon, who took on William Greatbatch as an apprentice in 1749, and Josiah Wedgwood as a partner in 1754, but with Daniel Bird, to whom John Turner was apprenticed in 1754. Incidentally, the fact that John Turner II was one of the witnesses to Whieldon's will in 1793[18] suggests a close relationship between Whieldon and the elder Turner.

In a letter of 31 January 1762 William Greatbatch told Wedgwood that he was going to set up business on his own, as Wedgwood had already done in 1759, and offered to supply him with teapots.[19] Early in 1762 he set up his factory at Lower Lane, Fenton, under a price agreement with Wedgwood to supply him with wares in the new taste set by the Continental factories and followed by Chelsea, Longton Hall, and the Whieldon partnership—of teapots and tureens in the form of cauliflowers, melons, and other vegetables. One of his letters to Wedgwood, undated, but probably written early in 1762, reads:

Lower Lane, Friday noon

Sir,

Please to send word by the Bearer whether we shou'd or not have sent you an apple Tpt. shou'd be glad to know if you wou'd have leaves on the side the same as use to be, send a Tpt. with Earl Bute on it, have sent Cash to pay for it.[20]

It is tempting to suggest that Greatbatch might have been working for Turner also at this date, and that he was the modeller of the Degg teapot. The date of that piece—March 1762—is about the date when Greatbatch set up business in Lower Lane. *The Connoisseur*, which first drew attention to the teapot, wrote of it:

> There may be traces of the same general influence as shows itself in the work turned out during the Whieldon-Wedgwood period; but then it was Whieldon who was the senior partner and ruling spirit. The pear shape of the teapot, the form and decoration of the moulded spout, and the relief ornament all appear more or less in the tortoise-shell and cauliflower teapots connected with his [Whieldon's] name.[21]

Greatbatch had only just left the Whieldon factory. His speciality was the 'Landskip teapot',[22] whose chief characteristic was the compression of a wealth of detail into the surface area—certainly a feature of the Degg teapot. Again, the blue colour with which the design is picked out was included in the palette of Greatbatch, or rather that of his enameller Courzen. Finally, we know that Greatbatch—probably early in 1762—was ordering a Lord Bute teapot from Wedgwood. Might this not have inspired the idea of a Lord Trentham teapot for John Turner?

Yet, with all these pointers, I cannot accept that the Degg teapot was modelled by Greatbatch. Comparing it with Greatbatch's known works, there is no one stylistic quirk which decisively stamps it as his work. The knop and handle are plainer than any of the known examples. The lips of Greatbatch's spouts are invariably cut off straight: that of the Degg teapot is shaped. The spout of the Degg teapot is moulded with a stylized leaf pattern, but not the 'wrapped leaf' pattern most frequently used by Greatbatch. The reticulated border at the foot of the teapot, and the miniature crazy-paving design round the rim, are not reproduced on any of the teapots accepted as Greatbatch's work. But overriding these differences in mannerism there is a more telling contrast to be made. Most of Greatbatch's known compositions are characterized by an erratic lyricism quite lacking in the contained, confident design of the Degg teapot. With Greatbatch, men and houses, animals and trees float about on the surface, as though they have just been landed on the Moon; on the Degg teapot the figure is firmly anchored and penned in by geometrical foliage.

The only certainty about Greatbatch's relation to Turner is that he was working for him in 1788, presumably as an outside potter supplying him with ware, for when bankrupted—first in February 1782 and again in April 1788—he was described in the *London Gazette* as 'William Greatbatch, potter, Stoke-on-Trent'.[23] It was after the second bankruptcy that he applied to Wedgwood for help, and was given the job of checking and receipting deliveries of clay to the factory.[24]

The best account of Greatbatch is a paper which the Honorary Secretary of the English Ceramic Circle, Mr Donald Towner, read to the Circle in 1961. William Absolon of Yarmouth, who decorated wares for Turner, has been equally royally treated by the President of the Circle, Mr A. J. B. Kiddell, in a paper of 1959. Absolon was born in 1751. He was apprenticed to William Manning as a potman and was made Freeman of Great Yarmouth in 1784. On 10 July 1784 he advertised in the *Norwich Mercury* that he had 'just returned from London with a large quantity of foreign and Salopian China, some Blue and Green-edge Table Services of two Sorts, and a Number of other Articles, which he is enabled to sell on the cheapest Terms. . . .' And according to Absolon's trade-card, he had 'a Manufactory for Enamelling & Gilding his Goods with Coats of Arms, Crests, Cyphers, Borders, or any other Device'. Absolon's work for such potters as Shorthose, Wilson, Davenport, Wedgwood, Turner, and others is easily recognizable. He made use of chocolate brown, a stony blue, and what Mr Kiddell calls 'a peculiar lustrous green'.[25] His borders are frequently blue or green (generally the latter), as suggested by the 1784 advertisement. He often signed his wares. A stoneware jug in the Norwich Museum bears both the impressed mark TURNER and Absolon's signature.[26] The Female Archers design in relief has been touched up in Absolon's distinctive palette, and the inscription 'A TRIFLE FROM YARMOUTH' written across the body of the jug. Absolon probably obtained his Turner wares from the London showrooms of Turner and Abbott in Fleet Street. He died in 1815.

Turner wares printed in underglaze blue are common.

The elder Mr Turner [writes Shaw] first employed a Blue Printer, who used wet Paper. His name was William Underwood, from Worcester; and he lived to a very advanced age. The Pattern Mr Turner used was the *willow*, designed by him from two oriental Plates, still preserved, and exhibited to the Author by Mr. W. Turner. The border remains, but the other parts are varied a little: the Cottage is altered in shape, and the Figures are less in the copy than in the originals.[27]

This is particularly interesting, in that it is the only suggestion we get, in any of the sources, that John Turner I was himself an artist. We know nothing further of William Underwood. An example of a Turner willow pattern (Plate 24b) is impressed with the hitherto unrecorded mark   TURNER   This enables us to date

MIST SOLE AGENT.

it fairly accurately to the period 1811–14, when James Underhill Mist was the Turners' London representative. A more fanciful design incorporating a corkscrew -trunked elephant (Plate 24a) was one of a series which included deer, gazelle, and rhinoceros designs.

Underglaze transfer-printing in other colours than blue is extremely rare in Turner pottery. Some plates marked TURNER, however, were decorated with black transfers engraved by John Aynsley of Lane End. Mr Donald Towner writes that it should not be assumed that Aynsley manufactured the ware on which his mark occurs;[28] and probably the Schreiber Collection plate engraved by Aynsley with his well-known 'Keep within compass' design[29] was made by Turner—it has a border of painted flowers similar in style to the painting on certain marked Turner examples.

Who was the flower painter? We do not know his name, but it is possible to speculate, on somewhat flimsy grounds, as to his origins. On 27 January 1953, a Worcester plate (Plate 28a) was sold at Sotheby's. It was catalogued as follows:

> Lot 84. A fine monochrome-decorated plate, from the *atelier* of James Giles, painted in Tournai style in the centre in carmine with an equestrian figure and a sheep in the foreground flanked by an urn on a pedestal, houses and trees in the background, the shaped gilt border with five carmine flower-sprays by the painter of the tulip with divergent petals, 9 in; Wall period.

The central scene may well have been painted by Fidellé Duvivier, who later worked for John Turner. It seems quite possible that the painter of the border— 'the painter of the tulip with divergent petals'—may also have worked for Turner at a later date. Compare the tulip on the Worcester plate with that on the pearlware plate (Plate 28b) in the Dublin Museum or that on the pearlware teapot (Plate 28c) in the author's collection. Compare also the rose on the Worcester plate with that on the Dublin plate; and the flower near the base of the handle of the teapot with that (to use military directions) at ten o'clock on the Worcester plate. Comparison should also be made between the Worcester decoration and that shown in the colour plate of the teapot. Obviously this point cannot be laboured; but it must at least be admitted as a possibility that the painter of the bifurcated tulips later worked for Turner, either, like Duvivier, in Staffordshire, or more probably in the London *atelier* of Andrew Abbott.

NOTES TO CHAPTER FOUR

[1] Referring to 'our new Shakespeare & Garrick', Wedgwood wrote to Bentley on 22 December 1777: 'You will see by looking under the shoulder of each that these heads are modeled [*sic*] by *Wm Hackwood*, but I shall prevent his exposing himself again now I have found it out. I am not certain that he will not be offended if he is refus'd the liberty of putting his name to the models which he makes quite new, & I shall be glad to have your opinion upon the subject. Mine is against any name being upon our articles besides W & B, & if you concur with me I will manage the matter with him as well as I can.' (*Letters of Josiah Wedgwood, 1772–1780*, ed. Lady Farrer, 1903, ii, 287–8.)

[2] Simeon Shaw, *History of the Staffordshire Potteries* (1829), p. 223.

[3] ibid., p. 229.

[4] *Ex. inf.* R. Oddy, Royal Scottish Museum, Edinburgh. (Letter of 18 September 1957.)

[5] '*Pilgarlic* or *Pill'd Garlic*. A 16th-century term for a bald-headed man, especially one whose hair had fallen off through disease, and had left a head that was suggestive of a piece of peeled garlic. Stow says of one getting bald: "He will soon be a peeled garlic like myself", and the term was later used of any poor wretch avoided and forsaken by his fellows, and, in a humorous or self-pitying way, of oneself.

' "After this feast we jogged off to bed for the night; but never a bit could poor pilgarlic sleep one wink, for the ever-lasting jingle of bells."—RABELAIS: *Pantagruel*, v, 7.' (Brewer's *Dictionary of Phrase and Fable*, 1962 edn, p. 709.)

[6] For an illustration of the Adams version, see William Turner, *The Collector* (1907), p. 46.

[7] William Chaffers, *Marks and Monograms* (1912 edn), p. 742.

[8] White's *History, Gazeteer and Directory of Staffordshire* (1834), p. 554.

[9] *Staffordshire Advertiser*, 30 March 1839.

[10] Josiah Wedgwood and Thomas Ormsbee, *Staffordshire Pottery* (1947), p. 42.

[11] R. G. Haggar, *Staffordshire Chimney Ornaments* (1955), p. 54.

[12] ibid., p. 132.

[13] G. E. Stringer, *New Hall Porcelain* (1949), p. 18.

[14] William Burton, *History and Description of English Earthenware and Stoneware* (1904), p. 156.

[15] For the information on William Greatbatch, I am indebted to the paper on the subject read to the English Ceramic Circle by Mr Donald Towner on 4 November 1961. (E.C.C. *Transactions*, vol. v, part iv.)

[16] Quoted ibid., p. 187.

[17] Simeon Shaw, *History of the Staffordshire Potteries* (1829), p. 156.

[18] P. W. L. Adams, *A History of the Adams Family* (1914), pp. 416–17. The wife of Whieldon, who was also an executor of the will, was Sarah Turner, 'daughter of John Turner of Cumberland Street, parish of St Marylebone, co. Middx., Esq.' Possibly she was related to John Turner II.

[19] E.C.C. *Transactions*, vol. v, part iv, p. 184.

[20] ibid., p. 185.

[21] *The Connoisseur*, May 1907, p. 51.

[22] E.C.C. *Transactions*, vol. v, part iv, p. 186.

[23] ibid., p. 192.

[24] loc. cit.

[25] E.C.C. *Transactions*, vol. v, part i, p. 59.

[26] This jug is illustrated, ibid., plate 48.

[27] Simeon Shaw, *History of the Staffordshire Potteries* (1829), p. 214.

[28] Donald Towner, *English Cream-Coloured Earthenware* (1957), p. 98.

[29] Illustrated by R. G. Haggar, *English Country Pottery* (1950), plate 16.

CHAPTER FIVE

Porcelain

IN THEIR ATTEMPT to imitate Chinese hard-paste porcelain English potters of the eighteenth century developed a material more sympathetic to the English genius —'artificial' or soft-paste porcelain. The warm, melting pastes of Bow, Chelsea, Derby and Worcester provided more congenial backgrounds for blowzy roses, dishevelled birds, and rustic lovers, than the blue, wickedly glittering surface of true china. Beside the *naïveté* and luxuriance of a red-anchor Chelsea dish, the perfectionist finish of a Chien Lung bowl seems cold, superficial, almost metallic. It is the difference between a Renoir and a Meissonier. In spite of this, certain English manufacturers continued to experiment, in the hope of discovering the hard-paste secret which had made the fortunes of Meissen and Sèvres. Like the alchemists' quest for the Philosopher's Stone, the search for the 'China Stone' which would transmute gross clay into the frail translucence of true porcelain became a mystic obsession. It was appropriate that the man who finally made the discovery—William Cookworthy of Plymouth—should have adopted an alchemical sign as his trade-mark.

The Chinese method of making hard-paste porcelain was described as early as 1717 by Francis d'Entrecolles, a Jesuit missionary with whose works Cookworthy was acquainted.[1] The two indispensable ingredients were *kaolin* (china clay) and *petuntse* (china stone). Cookworthy discovered these materials in Cornwall, opened a factory at Plymouth, and obtained a patent for his method on 17 March 1768. But conditions at Plymouth proved unsatisfactory, and two years later the factory was moved to Bristol. There Richard Champion, who already owned shares in the business, became manager, then proprietor. By a deed of assignment dated 6 May 1774 Cookworthy transferred to Champion the full patent rights. Champion in return pledged himself to pay a royalty to Cookworthy, thus doubling the cost of the materials. It was obvious that if the patent expired in 1782 Champion would be ruined, for the Staffordshire manufacturers would then be able to buy the clay and stone more cheaply, and there would be nothing to prevent them making hard-paste porcelain from the Cookworthy formula. In February 1775, therefore, Champion applied to Parliament to extend the patent for fourteen years beyond its original term.

Wedgwood opposed this extension, ostensibly with a characteristic argument of the Industrial Revolution, that it would create 'a Monopoly injurious to the Community at large'.[2] In addition, he claimed that Champion had no right to apply for an extension of a patent which he had merely purchased from the original inventor; and that in any case the patent granted to Cookworthy was itself invalid, as Cookworthy had not made an adequate specification of the principal processes involved.

Wedgwood canvassed support from the Staffordshire potters. On 10 May 1775, the *Petition of the Manufacturers of Earthen Ware in the County of Stafford* was presented to the House of Commons. While backing Wedgwood in his opposition, the other potters gave him a chaperon, to represent them and guard the general interests of the trade. This was John Turner. Possibly they felt that Wedgwood's animus against Champion was too extreme, and that by harnessing him with the level-headed Turner they would prevent an overstatement of their case. At any rate, their choice of Turner shows his eminence in the Potteries.

With the support of Edmund Burke, the Member for Bristol, Champion's bill passed the Commons by a majority of 49, without amendment. A similar success was to be anticipated in the Lords, where Champion's interests were represented by the Dukes of Portland, Manchester and Richmond, by the Marquis of Rockingham, and Earls Fitzwilliam, Effingham, and Berkeley. But the opposition, led by Earl Gower, was formidable, and Champion was obliged to make two concessions to appease it: he proposed that the Cornish materials should be available to other potters, but only for making earthenware, and that he would provide the House with a new specification of his methods of manufacture. Incorporating these amendments, the Bill was eventually passed towards the end of May 1775. Jubilant at their success, Wedgwood and Turner immediately set off for Cornwall. They left London on 29 May.

> The materials of course remaining free to be used by anyone, [wrote Wedgwood] I thought it would be proper to take a journey into Cornwall, the only part of the kingdom in which they are at present found, and examine upon the spot into the circumstances attending them,—whether they were to be had in sufficient quantities,—what hands they were in,—at what prices they might be raised, &c. &c. Mr Turner of Lane End agreed to accompany me thither; and the country being new to me, I took a few short minutes, in the chaises, of the various appearances of the country we passed through, &c. which might afford a little amusement at the time, & serve perhaps as an agreeeable companion in some future journey into the same places.[3]

It was typical of Josiah Wedgwood to find some occupation for himself during the long coach journey. His 'minutes' are written much in the style of Arthur Young, without the agricultural monomania, but with the same appreciation of formal beauty ('the great Brown himself could not trace a finer line of beauty') and the same sententious asides ('It is impossible to pass through these finely varied scenes, and comfortable haunts of men, without wishing to spend more time amongst them than these hurrying chaises will allow'). Curiously, no dates are given, only place-names and mileages. There is not a single mention of John Turner in the entire narrative, though whether this is indicative of Wedgwood's egotism or of Turner's dullness is not certain.

In Plymouth they met Henry Tolcher—'a lively old gentleman of near 90'— an alderman of the city, and an acquaintance of Dr Johnson. Tolcher offered to accompany them into Cornwall. At St Stephens they first saw the china stone. They took a joint lease of clay mines at Carlogus, at 4s. a ton,[4] and having thus concluded their business, they returned home, stopping on the way to view the ruins of Glastonbury. 'It was this momentous journey', Dr Bernard Watney has written, 'which determined the future of the potting industry in Staffordshire by making available comparatively inexpensive supplies of Cornish clay and stone.'[5]

As soon as Wedgwood arrived home he wrote to his partner Thomas Bentley:

We are to have a meeting of our potters, after which you shall hear from me again. . . . Mr Turner and I have concluded to set about washing some clay for ourselves and for others as soon as we can, if they chuse to have it, but at the same time to leave the raw clay open to all who chuse rather to prepare it for themselves, for I am firmly persuaded that an exclusive company, or rather an exclusive right in the clay in any company, or under any regulations whatever, would soon degenerate into a pernicious monopoly.[6]

A few days later, on 23 June 1775, he again wrote to Bentley:

We had a general meeting of the potters yesterday at Moretons on the Hill [Burslem] when we told them what had been done for their interests in London and in Cornwall. they were highly pleased with our negotiations and the generosity with which the Pottery at large had been treated. . . . I proposed a public experimental work [a research association] and they seemed to take the proposal very kindly, after I had cautioned them against a too precipitant change from a branch of business they were well acquainted with [the manufacture of Queen's ware or cream colour] to one in a great measure untried by anybody and quite unknown to themselves [the manufacture of porcelain] and we are to meet again in a fortnight to try if we can bring our plans to a tolerable degree of maturity.[7]

But, in fact, the research association fizzled out. The immediate cause of its dissolution was the failure of its members to agree whether the partners in company should pay separately or jointly.[8] But in any case Champion's patent made the manufacture of porcelain from his formula illegal, and the specification he submitted to Parliament was vague and ambiguous.[9] Wedgwood took his own advice and used the new materials not for making porcelain but for improving his creamware. The incorporation of the new clay and stone into both body and glaze produced a light, pale creamware which the other potters were quick to imitate. Wedgwood lost interest in china-making. When Champion, in 1780, took the extraordinary step of approaching his arch-enemy with the object of selling the patent, Wedgwood politely declined.[10]

But Turner never gave up the idea of becoming a porcelain manufacturer. It seems possible that he had experimented before 1780 with soft-paste. Mr W. B. Honey has attributed to him,[11] rather than to Thomas Turner of Caughley, a soft-paste mug marked TURNER impressed, now in the Hanley Museum (Plate 34a). Unlike Wedgwood, he was ready to listen to Champion's proposals.

The parliamentary struggle had crippled Champion financially. In August 1778 he assigned his property to trustees for the benefit of his creditors. A Commission of Bankruptcy, dated 29 August 1778, was declared against him, but was temporarily suspended on the same day, probably on the intervention of his influential friends, such as Edmund Burke and the Duke of Portland. Wedgwood wrote to his partner: 'Poor Champion, you may have heard, is quite demolished. It was never likely to be otherwise, as he had neither professional knowledge, sufficient capital, nor scarcely any real acquaintance with the materials he was working upon.'[12]

But Champion was not quite demolished. He continued to make porcelain at Bristol, though in greatly reduced quantities, until 1781. 'About 1777', writes Shaw, 'he sold the Patent to a Company in Staffordshire. Mr Samuel Hollins, Red China Potter of Shelton; Anthony Keeling Son-in-law of Enoch Booth, potter, Tunstall; John Turner, Lane End; Jacob Warburton, Son of William Warburton of Hot lane; William Clowes, potter of Pert Hill [Porthill]; and Charles Bagnall, potter, Shelton.'[13] We know that the date is wrong, for, as we have seen, Champion offered the patent to Wedgwood in 1780. But the facts receive some confirmation from Dr J. Aikin's *Description of the Country from Thirty to Forty Miles around Manchester* (1795):

> Shelton is an extensive place and has many considerable manufactories in it, among the rest, one which deserves particular notice, the porcelain or china manufactory carried on under the respectable firm of Hollins, Warburton, and Company. The

china made there is very little if at all inferior, especially in the colours, to that of the East Indies. . . . The ingenious Mr Champion of Bristol who discovered the art of making this porcelain, expended an ample fortune in the various trials. He had the good fortune, however, of bringing it to perfection and obtained a patent for the exclusive privilege of making it, which he sold to the above gentlemen for such a sum of money as enabled him to retire to America.[14]

This account is itself inaccurate. It was not Champion but Cook-worthy who discovered the art of hard-paste porcelain. But the mention of the purchase of Champion's patent by Hollins, Warburton and Company is striking corroboration of Shaw. Aikin would not be likely to mention Turner, who by 1795 had left the company. But that there was some association between Champion and Turner is suggested by Turner's later use of Bristol figure moulds (Plate 18).[15]

Of all the periods of Turner's life, this is the one which has been most mulled over by expert writers, as it brings him into the ambit of the porcelain connoisseur; yet it remains one of the most obscure. The train of events which it is possible to establish would seem to run as follows: after his failure to interest Wedgwood in the patent, in 1780, Champion had the idea of forming a large company in Stafford-shire. Besides running a communal factory, it would allow its members to make hard-paste porcelain in their own works on payment of a fine to the parent com-pany.[16] Wedgwood again opposed him, and the other potters were reluctant to form a company which would be burdened with the price Champion had to pay for the Cornish materials, when they could obtain them more cheaply themselves. Champion therefore abandoned this plan, and in 1781 moved from Bristol to Staffordshire to form a more limited company at Tunstall, presumably that de-scribed by Aikin and Shaw. In September 1781 Champion wrote to George Harrison, one of the executors of William Cookworthy, that 'I have now entered into an agreement with ten Potters only'[17]. Shaw's list contains only six potters: probably these were the most eminent of the ten. After the account of the sale of the patent, Shaw adds:

After this agreement, Mr Champion directed the processes of Manufacture for the Company, at the Manufactory of Mr Anthony Keeling at Tunstall; but when that gentleman (Mr Champion) removed to London, in 1782, a disagreement ensued among the partners; Mr Keeling and Mr John Turner withdrew, and they who continued to-gether engaged as managing partner, Mr John Daniel, Son of the person who introduced Plaster Moulds; and settled the manufactory at the New Hall, Shelton, only a short time previously erected by Mr Whitehead, of the Old Hall, Hanley; on which account the porcelain had the appellation of *New Hall China*.[18]

Shelton Hall (Plate 35) had been leased by John Turner in 1779, 'for 99 years, if Humphrey Palmer of Hanley shall so long live'.[19]

NOTES TO CHAPTER FIVE

[1] An English translation of the letters is given in William Burton, *Porcelain, its Nature, Art and Manufacture* (1906), pp. 84–122.

[2] Josiah Wedgwood, *A Memorial relative to a Petition from Mr Champion for the Extension of a Patent.* Quoted by Hugh Owen, *Two Centuries of Ceramic Art in Bristol* (1873), p. 121.

[3] Introduction to Wedgwood's Diary. *Proceedings* of the Wedgwood Society (1957).

[4] Wedgwood to Bentley, 21 July 1779: 'The mine rent of Mr Carthew's Growan Clay which is quite perfect and good is four shillings, per ton, and the expense of raising it is a trifle. Our taking a lease (Mr Turner and myself) of the clay at Carlogus reduced it to this price.' (Wedgwood MSS. E. 18911–28, 21 July 1779.)

[5] Dr Bernard Watney, *English Blue and White Porcelain* (1963), p. 121.

[6] E.18602–25 Wedgwood MSS. 18 June 1775.

[7] Wedgwood to Bentley, 23 June 1775. (*Letters to Josiah Wedgwood, 1772–1780*, ed. Lady Farrer, p. 116.)

[8] E. Meteyard, *The Life of Josiah Wedgwood* (1866), ii, 423.

[9] 'I enclose a copy of Champion's cunning and thrice cunning specification which outshines his former outshinings in the way of specifying.' (Wedgwood to Bentley, E.18624–25 Wedgwood MSS. 14 November 1775).

[10] Wedgwood to Bentley, 12 November 1780: 'Amongst other things, Mr Champion of Bristol has taken me up near two days. He is come amongst us to dispose of his secret, his patent, etc. Who would have believed it—has chosen me for his friend and confidant? I shall not deceive him for I really feel much for his situation—a wife and eight children to say nothing of himself to provide for, and out of what I fear will not be thought of such value here, the secret of china making. He tells me he has sunk £15,000 in this gulf and his idea is now to sell the whole art, mistery and patent for £6,000 and he is now trying a list of names I have given him of the most substantial and enterprising potters amongst us. . . .' (Quoted Dr John Thomas, *The Economic Development of the North Staffordshire Potteries since 1730, with Special Reference to the Industrial Revolution*, pp. 174–5.)

[11] *The Connoisseur*, January 1929, p. 45.

[12] Wedgwood to Bentley, 24 August 1778. Quoted E. Meteyard, *The Life of Josiah Wedgwood* (1866), ii, 422n.

[13] Simeon Shaw, *History of the Staffordshire Potteries* (1829), p. 201.

[14] J. Aikin, *Description of the Country from Thirty to Forty Miles around Manchester* (1795), p. 521.

[15] See F. Tilley, 'John Turner and the Bristol Moulds', *The Connoisseur*, June 1934, p. 390. Also B. Hillier, 'The Child Seasons: New Light on the Bristol-Turner Link', *The Connoisseur*, February 1964, p. 101.

[16] See R. J. Charleston, *The End of Bristol; the Beginning of New Hall: Some Fresh Evidence, The Connoisseur*, April 1956, p. 187.

[17] Champion to Harrison, 3 September 1781. Quoted ibid., p. 186.

[18] Simeon Shaw, *History of the Staffordshire Potteries* (1829), p. 201.

[19] Mr John Mallet of the Victoria and Albert Museum has gone to considerable trouble to trace the original of this document, but without success. It is quoted in part by G. E. Stringer, *New Hall Porcelain* (1949), p. 11.

CHAPTER SIX

The Gerverot Beaker

After Mr Turner had separated from the New Hall Company [wrote Shaw] he commenced the manufacture of porcelain, at Lane End; and one of the ornaments he made is now preserved by Broadhurst Harding, with truly laudable care and anxiety. It is a beaker, on which is enamelled, in brown colours, the whole interior of a Pottery. The celebrated modeller Gerverot designed it; and in quality it will still rank very high among English porcelain.[1]

THIS BEAKER HAS survived (Frontispiece and Plate 34b). It has an immaculate pedigree. In 1934 or 1935 it was bought by Major W. H. Tapp from Miss Lucy Evelyn Harding of Clayton, near Newcastle-under-Lyme. Miss Harding, a descendant of Broadhurst,[2] also owned the model of the New Hall factory (Plate 35), which she presented to Mr G. E. Stringer, who was then managing director of the factory. (Probably the New Hall model had also belonged to Broadhurst Harding.) The Gerverot beaker was damaged in an air raid on Major Tapp's Wimbledon home in 1944, but has been skilfully repaired. It was sold at Sotheby's on 27 June 1950, and is now in the American showrooms of the Antique Porcelain Company.

Messrs Reginald Haggar and Wolf Mankowitz, in their *Concise Encyclopaedia of English Pottery and Porcelain* (1950), suggest that Shaw may have made a mistake in ascribing the beaker to Gerverot, and that he really meant Mongenot, a Swiss modeller whose father was guillotined in the French Revolution.[3] This was a reasonable assumption, for Mongenot is known to have worked for William Adams, another of Wedgwood's eminent rivals. But, in fact, there is evidence from another quarter that Gerverot was working for John Turner in 1787, when the beaker was made.

Gerverot was a professional arcanist. He touted secret formulae and processes round the china factories of Europe. A detailed account of his movements is given by Heinrich Stegmann in his book *Die fürstlich Braunschweigische Porzellanfabrik zu Fürstenberg* (1893), based largely on documents at the Fürstenberg porcelain factory, of which Gerverot eventually became manager. The account of his life which follows is based almost entirely on Stegmann's account, of which no English

40

III. Pearl ware teapot, perhaps decorated by the Painter of the Tulip with Divergent Petals.
Mark: TURNER impressed. (See p. 30.) (Author's Collection.)

translation has been published. The sources of additional information are acknowledged.

Louis-Victor Gerverot was born on 8 December 1747 at Lunéville, where his father was music master to the dethroned King of Poland, Stanislaus Leszczinski. His father died while he was still a child, and his early education fell to his mother, who was of the d'Aubigny family. With the slender knowledge with which he was equipped by the Latin monastic school of his home town, he became an apprentice at the Sèvres porcelain factory, where his cousin, Marmet, was an inspector. He soon left Sèvres, however, and found employment as an apprentice bird-painter at the Lotharingian factory of Niderviller, where the production of true porcelain was being attempted with the help of German workers. Gerverot made the acquaintance of a son of the Baron Jean-Louis de Beyerlé, the director of the factory, and in return for a present of six carolines was given access to a book containing the secrets of the manufacture. He set aside every free hour to copy this manuscript from beginning to end. Then he set out for Germany.

The German factories welcomed the young Frenchman, who, with his Sèvres training, his pirated knowledge, and tales of Court life at Lunéville, knew how to make himself interesting. After a brief spell at Ludwigsburg, he travelled farther into the Ansbach region to the small town of Bruckberg, to which in 1762 the factory founded by the Margrave Frederick William of Brandenberg had just been moved. Here he tried out his gold-refining and colouring processes, with some success. His next destination was Höchst in the electorate of Mainz. By 1767, according to his own account, he had learnt all there was to be learnt at Höchst, and he made for North Germany. He was taken on as a flower-painter at Fürstenberg. There he made his mark, according to the painter Anton Jungesblut, by his skill and engaging manners, but the secrets of the factory were closely guarded. After seven months, therefore, he set off once more. In 1770 he was at Offenbach, near Frankfurt-on-Main. During a short stay at the Frankenthal factory he won several thousand guilders in the Mainz lottery. Full of extravagant plans, he travelled, in about 1771, to the Weesp factory in Holland, which had been founded by an Irish arcanist, Daniel MacCarthy, in 1757. The factory's director, the Count von Gronsfeld-Diepenbroek, gave him the post of laboratory assistant, experimenting with colours. But in 1773 the Count went bankrupt, and Gerverot was forced to look for another job. With his remaining capital he went to Schrezheim, near Ellwangen in Württemberg, and took a seven years' lease of a porcelain factory which the designer had left unfinished. He employed over twenty workers and himself acted as decorator, researcher, and book-keeper, and helped to man the kilns. A tankard painted with views of Ellwangen and illustrated by Pazaurek as a production of a factory there[4] is claimed by Stoehr as Schrezheim work done under the direction of Gerverot.[5] A famous rococo altar in faience made at Schrezheim (illustrated by Stoehr)[6] has been thought to be by Gerverot's own hand, but W. B. Honey considers it too early in style for that.[7]

The Schrezheim undertaking flourished. Demand was usually higher than production, and Gerverot bought white porcelain from Höchst for decoration, and helped out the factory at Bruckberg. His chief markets were German, Dutch, and Turkish. His trade-mark was a lion, but he also copied the marks of other factories where customers asked for them. At this time he made the friendship of Count Francis von Dettingen-Baldern, who was later to be of great service to him. He became a member of the Society for Moral and Agricultural Knowledge at Burghausen and of the Agricultural Society at Celle, and on 2 May 1775 Maximilian Joseph III of Bavaria appointed him to the Electoral Council.

After the expiry of his lease Gerverot attempted to obtain its renewal, but the terms offered were unacceptable. He emigrated again, this time to Holland, where at Oude-Loosdrecht the priest Johannes de Mol had set up a factory with a company of Amsterdam tradesmen. He became a partner. A Loosdrecht biscuit bust of Professor Jacob Willemsen of Middelburg, attributed to Gerverot, is illustrated by Riemsdijk.[8] Though technically competent, it is a mannered work in a debased rococo style. In 1782 de Mol died, and Gerverot was in danger of losing his and his wife's capital, which he had sunk in the venture. But Rendorp and Van der Hoop, who took over the concern, gave him back his money and sent him packing.

In 1777 Gerverot had married the well-dowried daughter of the Hamburg builder Salomon, brother of the Prussian general Salomon of Wesel. After leaving the Oude-Loosdrecht factory he went with her to Amsterdam. He could not obtain work there, however, and in 1786 he decided to go to England.

To the arcanist England offered two enticing prospects: an opportunity to sell the knowledge acquired at half the porcelain factories of Europe; and the chance of learning secrets of the English pottery manufacture, to sell abroad. After he had spent some time in London learning English, he advertised in the papers offering the secrets of porcelain to anyone who would form a partnership with him. He was approached by Wedgwood, who did not wish to commit himself to a partnership, but offered to buy the secret and to take on Gerverot as an employee in his factory. Gerverot, not to be outdone in wiliness, refused this offer,[9] and opened negotiations with John Turner. It was agreed that Gerverot should establish a porcelain factory on Turner's property at Lane End. As the materials had to be brought from a great distance, and many elaborate fittings installed, Gerverot only managed in nearly two years to bring four kilns to completion, and before the factory was completed the elder John Turner died. Because of Gerverot's failure to fulfil all the clauses of the agreement, he was sued by Turner's sons for breach of contract. From these entanglements he was rescued by the Marquis of Stafford, through the intervention of the Count von Dettingen-Baldern. Disgusted with the treatment he had met with, he left England for good.

He brought away his usual pirate's treasure. In England he had offered the secrets of porcelain. On the Continent he offered the secrets of stoneware. In 1788 he was in Cologne, setting up a factory for producing English stoneware with a number of wealthy tradesmen. With sixty to eighty workers, the factory made white and black stoneware, but though the wares had a good sale, persistent quarrels among the associates brought work to a halt and drove Gerverot away from Cologne in 1792. The Count von Dettingen-Baldern asked him to set up a stoneware factory at Sötern in his upper Rhenish county of Dachstuhl. He was also invited to establish factories at Mülheim on the Rhine, and at Hamm, but the outbreak of war between Germany and France put paid to these schemes.

The further activities of Gerverot do not greatly concern us. In 1797 he became manager of the Fürstenberg factory, with an annual income of 600 thalers. He remained in that respectable position for seventeen years. There he put into practice some of the ideas he had acquired in England. On the artistic side he now favoured neo-classicism, and made busts and medallions similar to those of Wedgwood and Turner.[10] He also imported some of the social liberalism of Wedgwood and Turner: he instituted a pension scheme for the workmen, and, like Wedgwood, planted flowers round his factory.

On 18 August 1807 the Grand Duchy of Brunswick, in which the Fürstenberg factory was situated, was incorporated in the new Napoleonic kingdom of Westphalia. Gerverot, as a Frenchman, was patronized by King Jérôme, but when the Duke of Brunswick was restored in 1814 he was dismissed without a pension as a collaborator. He was now 67, his wife 72. He was accused of financial malpractices, and the long investigation which followed delayed his departure until 1816. He was cleared, however, given a present of 200 thalers, and became manager of the factory at Wrisbergholzer, a position he held until 1826, when he finally retired. He died at Bevren in 1829, the year in which Simeon Shaw's description of the Gerverot beaker was published.

By Stegmann's account, then, Gerverot arrived in England not earlier than 1786, and left in 1788. The beaker is inscribed in one panel 'Lane End juin [*sic*]

1787', and, on the base, 'Lane End july 1787'. As Shaw states, it depicts 'the whole interior of a Pottery'. There are two panels, surrounded by primitive oil-gilt cartouches. Both panels show *bambini* at work, in one case turning a pot, in the other, loading a kiln with saggars. Between the panels are painted the Prince of Wales's feathers. Over a doorway in the kiln-loading scene is the enamelled inscription 'Duvivier pxt'.

The style is unmistakably that of Fidellé Duvivier, one of a family of decorators who came to England from Tournai. He was born in the parish of St Brice-Tournai on 6 August 1740, the son of Jacob Franciscus Duvivier.[11] Probably he was apprenticed to François Peterinck of the Tournai factory, and it seems likely that he was at the James Giles *atelier* in London in the seventeen-sixties, when he may well have decorated the Worcester plate illustrated in Plate 28a. In 1769 he was engaged for four years by William Duesbury of Derby, as a 'porcelain painter and [painter of] roses'. (His son Peter Joseph was baptized in St Alkmund's Church, Derby, on 20 March 1771.) De Chavagnac and De Grollier state in their *Histoire des Manufactures françaises de Porcelaine* (1906) that he was working at Sceaux, outside Paris, in 1775.[12] His subsequent movements are uncertain. Major Tapp, his assiduous biographer, has suggested that he was at Worcester from 1777 to 1780, on the grounds that a part tea service in the Luton Museum, signed by him, was made at Worcester. But, in fact, the tea service is far more likely to be New Hall (it is catalogued as such by the museum); Duvivier was certainly working for New Hall in 1790, when he wrote to Duesbury's son from Hanley Green asking for casual employment. The original registers of Hanley Green Church were destroyed in Chartist riots, and those that are preserved are hastily made transcripts; but Fidellé Duvivier appears to have been buried there on 12 October 1817. It is surely more than a coincidence that Broadhurst Harding, father of the man who owned the Gerverot beaker when Shaw described it, was buried (in the same year) in the same church.

Any discussion of the Gerverot beaker must be accompanied by mention of a more experimental piece, a bowl in the British Musuem, also painted in sepia, with oil-gilt borders (Plate 34c). The inscription on the base of the bowl, as on that of the beaker, is 'Lane End july 1787', and the calligraphy is so similar as to leave no doubt that the writer was the same. The glaze of the bowl, which is dull and lustreless, has crazed badly and subsequently become stained with grease. Stegmann's account suggests that Gerverot had difficulty in obtaining the materials he needed. Shaw, in his *Chemistry of Pottery*, states that 'the common porcelains of Champion and Turner had been proved refractory in the oven'.[13] Even the

Gerverot beaker, a much more finished piece than the British Museum bowl, is marred by minor imperfections. The paste is spotted, and the oil gilding, as on the bowl, has in places rubbed off, recalling Shaw's comment on the Turners' 'shining blue' pottery:

> The specimen preserved is a pint Cup, which, had the ability of the Gilder been as well employed in preparing his gold, as in the execution of the Pattern, would have equalled any of the rich Gilding of this day of the Artists employed by Mr Spode, Mess Daniels, Mess Ridgeways, or Mr Minton.[14]

Owing to its dull and scratched glaze, the British Museum bowl has always been catalogued as soft-paste porcelain.[15] But recent X-ray diffraction analysis has shown the presence of the mineral mullite, thus indicating that the bowl is a true hard-paste porcelain.[16] Although it has not been possible to have the Gerverot beaker analysed, it seems probable that this, too, in spite of its fairly soft appearance, is of hard-paste composition—a probability converted into near-certainty by Stegmann's assertion that 'Gerverot worked with John Turner as a pioneer of hard porcelain manufacture' (*Fabrikation des Hardporzellans*).[17] The only instance of Gerverot's piracy specifically mentioned by Stegmann was the copying of formulae at Niderviller—a hard-paste factory.

NOTES TO CHAPTER SIX

[1] Simeon Shaw, *History of the Staffordshire Potteries* (1829), p. 204.

[2] Miss Harding was the granddaughter of Wingfield Harding, Broadhurst's son, a china manufacturer who died on May 20 1858 and not, as Jewitt states, in 1856. Wingfield's sons, W. and J. Harding, took over the New Hall factory in 1862.

[3] R. G. Haggar and W. Mankowitz, *Concise Encyclopaedia of English Pottery and Porcelain* (1957), p. 95.

Mongenot's obituary appeared in the *Staffordshire Advertiser* of 5 March 1814:

'DIED. Lately, at Tunstall, in the Potteries, in his 46th year, Joseph Mongenot, a native of Switzerland, but resident in England the last 26 years. He was an artist of considerable merit in the engraving, modeling, and painting departments, and his pen drawings will long remain treasured-up in the cabinets of the curious, as monuments of human ingenuity. He occasionally exercised his profession in London, Birmingham, and the principal towns in England, and maintained himself with respectability; for the last two years he resided in the Potteries where his productions in the engraving branch are well known. He had long been afflicted with what the faculty deemed a liver complaint, consequently was much reduced in circumstances—and we must relate to the honour of his brother artists in the Potteries, that they came feelingly, and liberally forward to smoothen the pillow of affliction, and committeed his remains to the dust with every token of true respect. His father was an officer in the French Service prior to the Revolution, but was guillotined at Montpellier, during the sanguinary reign of Robespierre.'

In spite of certain discrepancies, Joseph Mongenot can surely be identified with the 'Joseph Monglott' referred to in William L. Turner, *William Adams, An Old English Potter* (1904), p. 25:

'The principal modellers were William Adams himself, and Joseph Monglott. The latter was "an artist of merit in modelling and purity". He was a native of Switzerland, and came to England in 1785. Mr Adams induced him to live at Tunstall, and he became the principal modeller at the Greengates factory, where he conceived and prepared the designs for the bas-reliefs of the Sacrifices to the Apollo Belvedere; Diana and Pomona; also, those emblematical of the Arts and Sciences; the two subjects of Females and Cupid conversing; Nymphs dancing; Aphrodite in her car drawn by swans on clouds (after Le Brun); and many others. It might be said, as Wedgwood had his Flaxman, that Adams had his Monglott.'

[4] See W. B. Honey, *European Ceramic Art* (1952), p. 553.

[5] A. Stoehr, *Deutsche Fayencen und deutsches Steingut* (1919), p. 248.

[6] loc. cit.

[7] W. B. Honey, *European Ceramic Art* (1952), p. 272.

[8] *Oud-Holland*, xxxiii (1915), p. 178.

[9] At least, so Stegmann says. But in view of Gerverot's extensive knowledge of the Wedgwood factory, relayed to the directors of Fürstenberg (see *Sprechsaal für Keramik, Glas und Emil*, 1883, Nos. 14 and 15, in which Stegmann prints these letters), it seems possible that Gerverot worked for Wedgwood at some time.

[10] One is illustrated by Geoffrey Wills in *Apollo*, February 1959, p. 46.

[11] I am indebted for some of my information on Fidellé Duvivier to the two articles on him by the late Major W. H. Tapp, which appeared in *Apollo*, December 1940 and March 1941.

[12] At p. 369.

[13] Simeon Shaw, *Chemistry of Pottery* (1837), p. 422.

[14] Simeon Shaw, *History of the Staffordshire Potteries* (1829), p. 222.

[15] R. L. Hobson, describing this bowl in the British Museum catalogue (p. 154), says: 'The paste is soft enough to yield to a steel blade, and the glaze, which is dull and lustreless, has crazed badly and subsequently become stained with greasy matter.'

[16] *Ex. inf.* G. H. Tait, letter of 16 September 1964.

[17] *Sprechsaal für Keramik, Glas und Emil* (1883), No. 14.

CHAPTER SEVEN

The French Revolution

'I KNOW YOU WILL rejoice with me in the glorious revolution which has taken place in France,' wrote Josiah Wedgwood to Dr Erasmus Darwin in July 1789. 'The politicians tell me that as a manufacturer I shall be ruined if France has her liberty, but I am willing to take my chance in that respect, nor do I yet see that the happiness of one nation includes in it the misery of its next neighbour.'[1] Wedgwood was a typical disciple of the Enlightenment. As a dissenter he had a natural radical bias. He offended his Liverpool business friends by his strong anti-slavery views; his propagandist medallion of a chained negro with the inscription 'Am I not a Man and a Brother?' was adopted as the seal of the Slave Emancipation Society.[2] During the American War of Independence he was openly pro-American, and produced jasper portraits of Washington and Franklin. He admired Voltaire and Rousseau (though, as a good businessman, he made busts of them in black to please the clergy). On the advice of Lady Mary Wortley Montagu he had his children inoculated against smallpox—the disease by which he himself had been crippled in childhood—at a time when inoculation was still thought to be flying in the face of Providence.[3] He was the Enlightened Despot of the Potteries.

It was not only his liberalism, however, that enabled Wedgwood to view the Revolution with such complacency. He knew that the loss of the French market would not in reality ruin him. He had too many other strings to his bow. He had established markets in many European countries, and shipped wares to the Far East as well. 'Mr Wedgwood's manufactures are in such repute in China', said his high-flown obituary in the *Staffordshire Advertiser*, 'that the houses of the principal mandarins are decorated with his wares.'[4] And if all else failed, his domination of the English market would save him from absolute ruin.

The situation of the Turners was very different. Apart from Holland and Belgium, France was, so far as we know, their only foreign market, and their share of the English market was far smaller than Wedgwood's.

In the same month as his exultant letter to Erasmus Darwin, Josiah Wedgwood received news from his son of the effect of the Revolution on his business:

JOSIAH WEDGWOOD JUNIOR TO JOSIAH WEDGWOOD SENIOR

Etruria, July 28 1789.

Messrs Verlingen & son of Boulogne owe us £380. I will translate a part of their letter of 24 inst. 'We are Sir in very unfortunate circumstances, the crisis that France & of consequence Commerce, suffers at present, the horrid misery which ravages all the provinces & which influences all conditions, has totally suppressed circulation & sale, an over flow of goods of which we have laid in too great a stock, calculating the future sales of this year in proportion to those which last years plenty had produced & in short the delay of payments which we ourselves have suffered under, make it impossible for us to fulfil our engagements with the exactness upon which we have untill now piqued ourselves. Therefore Sir we beg you to consider our situation in the payment of what we owe you & be perswaded that as soon as the sales are renewed we will exert ourselves to the utmost to satisfy you; trust our probity & the delicacy of our sentiments. We have always endeavoured to merit the esteem of our correspondants, happy if we have obtained yours. It is at this moment especially that we have the greatest need of it & that we shall without doubt congratulate ourselves on having gained your good will & opinion.'[5]

The Turners apparently experienced similar difficulties in obtaining money owed to them by the French. William Turner visited France in an attempt to retrieve the situation. When exactly he went, and what exactly happened to him there, are not clear. The sources contradict themselves and each other. The longest account is that of Henry Wedgwood:

Mention has been made of the market which the elder Turner made for his goods in France, and this market was earnestly cultivated by his two sons and successors. Having means at their command, they committed themselves to a large amount of credit in that country. There was no fear of miscarriage, money had always been forthcoming, and by the past they judged of the future. Things, however, got into a very disturbed state, bills due upon French tradesmen were dishonoured, and there was no such thing as getting a settlement for goods sent out by English manufacturers. The Turners had an exceedingly large amount owing to them by these French merchants, which if not paid meant ruin to our Staffordshire potters. Matters became no better, and a gloomier look-out seemed pending, William Turner, therefore, resolved on visiting France for the recovery of their debts before political events should make it impossible to obtain them which appeared quite likely.

It was the year 1789 when he set out, and on arriving in Paris he found affairs much worse than he expected. There was no business doing, or to be done, least of all were there any debts to be collected from a people who were repudiating everything. Hoping perhaps against hope, considering that their future was at stake, Turner stayed in the city longer than was safe. One day being out in the streets on the same hopeless expedition, the frenzy broke out among the citizens for taking of the Bastile. In this mighty rabble poor Turner was caught, and despite himself was hurried along in the direction of that old fortress. All who were taken in this way by the mob, no matter what may have been their condition, were compelled to assist in the work in hand. Picks were distributed, and one of them was put in the hands of William Turner, and he was forced to work with the rest of the populace in demolishing that ancient enemy of the French people. Nor was he allowed to go his own way until picks and pikes had done their work and the Bastile was taken. But when set at liberty, where could he escape to, he was hemmed in on every side and there was no leaving the country.? There was now more fear of Turner paying the final debt than his collecting his temporal debts. Soon after his adventure at the Bastile he was apprehended in the streets on suspicion of being a Dutch spy. On this charge he was hurried before one of the Paris tribunals, and his defence being disbelieved he was either remanded or sentenced to death. However, there can be no doubt what his end would have been had he not been successful in making his case known to the Marquis of Stafford, who was our ambassador at Paris, and had not yet left the French Court. By the representations of the Marquis, Turner escaped with his life, but their fortune was gone.[6]

Turner's obituary in the *Staffordshire Advertiser* had given a similar account:

At the breaking out of the French Revolution, Mr Turner happened to be in France, where he sustained heavy pecuniary losses in consequence of being taken prisoner as a Dutch spy, on which charge he was tried and acquitted by a mock tribunal. Afterwards the Revolutionists compelled him to work with a pick in demolishing the Bastile. He ultimately owed his liberty, and perhaps his life, to the interposition of the late Duke of Sutherland, our ambassador at the court of Paris at that time.[7]

Simeon Shaw makes no mention of the Bastille, or the suspicion of Turner's being a Dutch spy:

Mr W. Turner happened to be in Paris when the reign of terror was most awful; and the application for Moneys due to him, was returned by incarceration and several examinations—not very pleasant to the free-born Englishman.—Indeed, he acknowledges, that he owes his liberty, and most probably his life, to the interference of the present Marquis of Stafford; whose Physician, Dr James, and Secretaries, Messrs Erskine and Hutchinson, were most busily employed to obtain his liberty. And, when, subsequently, the gens d'arme' brought his Passport, he witnessed the infatuation of a bastard freedom, in the most haughty rejection of the douceur Mr Turner liberally offered the bearer of so welcome a document.[8]

Shaw's account, the earliest of the three and the only one based on the direct testimony of William Turner himself, is the most convincing. The names of the agents of liberation are given. The circumstantial detail of the last sentence has the ring of first-hand authority. The *Staffordshire Advertiser*, followed by Henry Wedgwood, may well have involved Turner in the most famous act of the Revolution—the fall of the Bastille—simply to give additional popular interest to the story. Shaw would be deterred from any such fabrication by the knowledge that William Turner and probably also the Marquis of Stafford would read his account.

There is nothing improbable in the accounts of Turner's imprisonment. Since 1786 there had been growing resentment against English potters in France. In that year a commercial treaty was concluded between England and France, ending the high protective duties which had existed throughout the eighteenth century to the disadvantage of both countries and the profit of smugglers. In place of the high duties, an *ad valorem* duty of 12 per cent was to be paid on pottery, porcelain, and glass. The French manufacturers did badly out of this transaction. The *Chambre de Commerce* of Normandy, in its *Observations sur la Traité de Commerce entre la France et l'Angleterre* (1786), complained that 'Our potteries cannot escape a notable prejudice; the low price of coals in England enables the English to undersell us in these articles 25 per cent; considerable changes have already arrived at Rouen.'[9]

At Bordeaux, in 1787, Arthur Young observed: 'Warehouses of English goods are opened. The article which has hitherto sold the best, and quickest, is that of the Staffordshire potteries.[10] In the following year he visited the great Fair of Guibray, and 'found the quantity of English goods considerable, hard and queen's ware . . . A dozen of common plain plates, 3 livres and 4 livres for a French imitation, but much worse . . . a dozen with blue or green edges; English 5 livres 5 sous.'[11]

In Rouen the influx of English ware threw 1,500 families out of work. It is not surprising, therefore, that we hear of potters among the leading revolutionaries. A porcelain manufacturer, Olivier[12] of the Rue de la Roquette, Paris, incited his workmen 'in the most lurid and provocative terms'[13] to take part in the Réveillon Riots of April 1789, the first great popular outbreak of the Revolution.

So far as we know, William Turner was the only English potter who went to France in the Revolution. As such, he would be an inviting scapegoat, a chance for the French to revenge themselves on the English earthenware industry. Turner probably found himself completely out of his depth. An unimaginative potter, who had spent his life in the most doggedly provincial of English towns, he was suddenly precipitated into the greatest imbroglio of eighteenth-century history, and the most sophisticated city in Europe. Transposing female into male, plural into singular, amorous into political, we might apply to him Duff Cooper's malicious remark on Fanny Burney and her sister, who were suddenly, also as a result of the Revolution, brought into contact with the philandering *émigrés* of Juniper Hall[14]—Madame de Stael, Talleyrand, and the rest:

Prim little figures, they had wandered out of the sedate drawing rooms of *Sense and Sensibility*, and were in danger of losing themselves in the elegantly disordered alcoves of *Les Liaisons Dangereuses*.[15]

To what condition did the loss of their debts and French market reduce the Turners? Henry Wedgwood's narrative suggests that it was fatal to them:

By the representations of the Marquis, Turner escaped with his life, but their fortune was gone. Henceforth, with all their ingenuity, their [*sic*] is nothing but failure before the two brothers. There was no redeeming a fortune lost upon a forlorn country. France swallowed up the largest portion of their means, and bankruptcy swallowed up the rest. Their manufactory was closed; their models and moulds disposed of by the hammer of the auctioneer; and themselves given over to little better than poverty.[16]

Shaw's account is substantially the same:

Their further progress was prevented, and themselves completely ruined, by the political convulsions in France at the era of the reign of terror; their principal market was destroyed, their property confiscated, and themselves unexpectedly reduced, from a near prospect of great affluence to a state of comparative indigence.[17]

The fact remains that the Turner factory continued to produce pottery, and in considerable quantities, after the Revolution. So either the Turners made a new start with their depleted capital, with some success, or Shaw and Wedgwood are wrong in their estimate of the damage, or in their chronology. It is difficult to determine at what date William Turner was in Paris. Henry Wedgwood states: 'It was 1789 when he set out.' This is not unlikely. As early as July 1789 Verlingen and Son were informing Josiah Wedgwood that they were unable to honour their debts. The Turners withdrew more money from their London partnership in 1788–9 than at any other time.[18] Against this, 1789 is the obvious date which an amateur historian would light upon in discussing the French Revolution. So far as most Englishmen were concerned, the Fourteenth of July *was* the Revolution. Again, Henry Wedgwood later mentions 'the revolutionary tribunals', which would suggest a later date: the first revolutionary tribunal was established on 17 August 1792.

Certainly that is the period suggested by Simeon Shaw's account: 'Mr W. Turner happened to be in Paris *when the reign of terror was most awful.*' But Shaw, too, is an amateur historian, and not an impeccably accurate one. If taken literally, his statement would mean that Turner was in Paris in the 1790s—though not after 1792, when the English Ambassador returned to England. And though he is a sufficiently unprecise historian to make it possible that he used the expression 'reign of terror' merely as a more emphatic alternative to 'the French Revolution', we again have evidence from the account books of the London partnership that the Turners were withdrawing capital at this time.[19]

A totally different date for the Turners' catastrophe is suggested by William Burton:

> The business of the Turner family, obviously an important and extensive one, was seriously damaged and finally crippled by Napoleon's continental successes, as large consignments of their pottery were seized in several of the continental ports. William Turner crossed to Paris in an attempt to secure some of the outstanding debts, and was arrested as a spy and thrown into that dread prison, La Force. He was released after a time, through the representations of the British Ambassador, and returned to England, but these losses had so undermined their commercial position that the brothers felt compelled to give up the struggle, and they retired from business in 1803.[20]

Burton's works are the last which can be treated as in any way source-books for the history of the Turners. *A History and Description of English Earthenware and Stoneware*, his first book, was written in 1904, when men who had known William Turner were still living. He must have had access to some such source, or to strong local traditions—he lived in the Potteries—for he gives us information not to be found in any of the original sources. Only Burton tells us—accurately, as it transpires from Mrs Young's collection—that 'Turner made an abundance of cameos, seals, beads, shoe buckles, ear-rings, and suchlike articles, all most skilfully wrought, which were used by the Birmingham metal mounters and which are often confounded with those made by Wedgwood'.[21] Only Burton mentions 'an old tradition in the potteries that John Turner sacrificed many an ovenful of ware to secure the success of his trials and experiments'.[22] Only Burton relays the tradition that John Turner made a complete reproduction of a banquet of pastries which was, on completion, 'exhibited at one of the inns at Lane End, where it made a nine-days' wonder for the countryside'.[23] And Burton's is the earliest reference to the Ray bust.[24] However, the quotation above seems to confuse two separate periods in the factory's history. Together with the new idea that Napoleon's Continental System was the cause of ruin, and the new information that Turner was imprisoned in La Force, there are unmistakable echoes of the earlier accounts of Turner's adventures in the Revolution.

Sifting through the four sources—Shaw, the *Staffordshire Advertiser* obituary, Henry Wedgwood, and William Burton—it is possible, by comparison with the Turner-Abbott accounts and other morsels of independent witness, to select the most plausible evidence and suggest a possible sequence of events. Probably the Turners, like Wedgwood, were in difficulties by 1789, through the non-payment of debts by the French. The London account books give weight to this idea. But the earliest and most convincing source—Simeon Shaw—suggests that it was not until later that Turner went to Paris, perhaps in 1792, when the brothers altogether withdrew from the London partnership. This dating would rule out the Bastille incident, which in any case sounds mythopoeic. Turner was arrested, perhaps on the pretext of his being a Dutch spy, but in fact because he was an English potter. Possibly he was imprisoned in La Force, as Burton alone records. He was released through the intervention of the Marquis of Stafford. He was unsuccessful in collecting the outstanding debts. As for Burton's account, the Napoleonic blockade may well have been the *coup de grâce* to an already tottering business.

NOTES TO CHAPTER SEVEN

[1] Wedgwood to Darwin, July 1789. (*Correspondence of Josiah Wedgwood 1781–1794*, ed. Lady Farrer, 1906, p. 92.)

[2] One of these Wedgwood anti-slavery medallions is in the family collection of Mrs Young. This may mean that Turner's sympathies lay the same way.

[3] In 1774 inoculation was prohibited in Oxford by the Vice-Chancellor and Mayor (J. M. Thompson, *Lectures on Foreign History*, 1954, p. 359).

[4] *Staffordshire Advertiser*, 8 August 1795.

[5] *Correspondence of Josiah Wedgwood, 1781–1794*, ed. Lady Farrer (1906), p. 96.

[6] *Staffordshire Sentinel*, 8 February 1879.

[7] *Staffordshire Advertiser*, 11 July 1835.

[8] Simeon Shaw, *History of the Staffordshire Potteries* (1829), p. 223.

[9] Arthur Young, *Travels in France*, ed. Constantia Maxwell (1929), p. 324.

[10] ibid., p. 326.

[11] ibid., p. 102.

[12] Olivier was principally a manufacturer of stoves. A late eighteenth-century catalogue of these, preserved in the Sir John Soane Museum, London, is entitled, *Collection de dessins de poêles de forme antique et moderne de l'invention et de la manufacture de sieur Ollivier, rue de la Roquette, faubourg Saint Antoine*. There are several marked or well-documented specimens of the stoves at the Sèvres Museum, including one in the form of the Bastille, given by Olivier to the Convention in 1790. These stoves are painted in enamel colours, as are his drug-pots, of which marked specimens are also at Sèvres. Olivier

also made porcelain models of the Bastille (see 'La Bastille et les faïenciers' in *La Révolution Française, i* [1881], 116–18).

[13] George Rudé, *The Crowd in the French Revolution* (1959), p.43.

[14] For an account of the French *émigrés'* life at Juniper Hall, Surrey, see the Duchess of Sermoneta, *The Locks of Norbury* (1940), pp. 60–66, 70–73, and Constance Hill, *Juniper Hall* (1904).

[15] Duff Cooper, *Talleyrand* (1938), p. 64.

[16] *Staffordshire Sentinel*, 8 February 1879.

[17] Simeon Shaw, *History of the Staffordshire Potteries* (1829), p. 223.

[18] See p. 63 of the present book.

[19] loc. cit.

[20] William Burton, *Josiah Wedgwood and His Pottery*, 1922, p. 154.

[21] ibid., pp. 152–3.

[22] William Burton, *History and Description of English Earthenware and Stoneware* (1904), p. 154.

[23] ibid., p. 156.

[24] loc. cit.

CHAPTER EIGHT

The London Partnership

So LITTLE HAS been known, until now, of Turner's partners Abbott and Mist that Colonel Grant, in *The Makers of Black Basaltes*, wrote in scholarly bewilderment that 'it cannot be authoritatively stated that there were not in fact two distinct Abbotts and two Mists'[1]—a speculation worthy of the Gothick chronicler of a haunted abbey. To add to the confusion, Chaffers, in his *Marks and Monograms*, misread the impressed mark 'Jas. Mist' as 'Jos. Mist', and thus wrongly christened Turner's London agent Joseph Mist.[2] Happily, the Abbott Papers, preserved in the Dorset Record Office—an unlikely harbour for the archives of a London dealer in Staffordshire pottery—give at least enough information about both men to rid us of these ambiguities. And for the history of the Turner factory, they are the most valuable primary source we have.

Andrew Abbott was born at Bradford Abbas, Dorset, in 1743, the eldest son of Thomas Abbott. He had one sister, Elizabeth, and three brothers—Isaac, who became a woolstapler at Piddletrenthide; James, who was in the turtle trade, and John (1748–1832), a Quaker merchant who emigrated to America. When Andrew died in 1819, his daughter Hannah wrote to her Uncle John asking for an account of her father's ancestors and early life. He replied:

My dear Niece, it is impossible for me to give thee any satisfactory account of our father's predecessors, as my father was deceased before I had much recollection of him and my not having heard from my Mother, anything relating to his forefathers.

Thy dear father was put an apprentice (while I was young and at school) to a person of the name of Oaks (or Noaks) at Yetminster, to learn the trade of a Maltster, but before the expiration of his time he ran away, and got as far as Salisbury (on his way to London) where he was overtaken by his master and brought back, served out his time, after which he went to live with a Magistrate at Sherborne, after some time he went to London, and was in distress, so much so that he had to sell his buckles for support, before he could find employment, he got into employment of gilding of black tea ware, after that he got a better place by being clerk to a person of the name of William Bacchus,[3] who kept a Queen's ware warehouse in Thames Street, London— in which station he was when I left England in the year 1768. At my return after an absence of 17 years he was in partnership with John Turner in Fleet Street . . . such the short is the best of my recollections . . . I am, with sincerest affection and love

thy Antient Uncle
JOHN C. ABBOTT.

Some parts of this account are confirmed by other sources. The apprenticeship books at the Public Record Office, London, record the apprenticeship of Andrew Abbott to Edward Noak of Yeatminster, [*sic*] Dorset, on 9 August 1754, for a period of seven years having effect from 19 July, in the sum of £2. Supporting evidence for Abbott's acquaintance with Bacchus is contained in two letters of 1814. In that year Abbott's former clerk, Trais, was looking for a new job, and wrote to him, from Fetter Lane (14 November 1814):

> I called at Messrs Backhouse [*sic*] & Green to see Mr Ogden. I have been there twice, the first time I saw Mr Backhouse, the second time I see Mr Green who told me Mr Backhouse was gone into Staffordshire butt was expected home in a week & Desired me to Call when he came Home. I think Perhaps they may have some oppening for me. I shall feel much Obliged if you would recommend me to them. Either to Travell for them or to be with the Workhouse to take Orders.

In a letter of 14 December 1814, Trais wrote:

> I am told the Warehouse in Thames Street that was Mr Ogdins is now Messrs Bacchus & Green. Mr Green I believe is a Nephew to Mr Green who is a Partner with Mr Pellet[4] at the Falcon Glass Hos.

Trais, in fact, joined Jackson & Co. of Red Lion Street instead.

John Abbott's final statement, that in 1785 his brother was in partnership with John Turner in Fleet Street, is confirmed by an advertisement for the firm of Turner and Abbott in the *Morning Herald and Daily Advertiser* of 31 January 1785 (see p. 59).

In 1780 Abbott was admitted to the freedom of the City of London. Until the middle of the nineteenth century the freedom of the City was compulsory for all who traded within its boundaries, and could be obtained only through one of the City livery companies. Then, as now, there were three methods of admission: by patrimony, which was the right of the sons of freemen; by apprenticeship, which followed the serving of an apprenticeship to a freeman; and by redemption (purchase). Abbott's admission was by redemption. The official entry in the Chamberlain's records (the Chamberlain was John Wilkes) reads:

> Andrew Abbott of Fleet Street, London, chinaman and Potter, made free by *redemption*, the fifth day of December 1780.[5]

IV. Two jugs and a mug marked 'Turner's Patent' in red. (See pp. 21–22.) (Mrs Eric Young.)

He was admitted as a member of the Carpenters' Company: this does not necessarily mean that he practised the carpenter's trade for the essential requirement was
not that he should belong to the company of his trade, but to any company at all—
and there was no Worshipful Company of Potters.[6]

It is interesting to note that Abbott is referred to as a potter as well as a 'china-
man' (china dealer). There is in the Glaisher Collection at the Fitzwilliam Museum,
Cambridge, a dark-red baking-dish of late eighteenth-century type decorated with
combed slip, marked 'Abbott Potter' impressed. Possibly Abbott was a potter in his
own right before he became John Turner's partner. His account books show that
he was a partner in the firm of Abbott and Smee, who were described as 'Potters'
(Prince's Street, Lambeth) in *Kent's Directory* of 1797, and as 'Brown-Stone potters'
(Vauxhall) in *Holden's Triennial Directory* of 1799.

December 1780, the month in which Abbott became a freeman, is also, signi-
ficantly, the first month in which any hint is given of an association between himself and John Turner. In Abbott's private account book for that month he records
the following debt to Samuel Emery, Turner's brother-in-law:

Dec. 13. Cash to Pay Coach down to Brewood. 2. 12. 6.

What the purpose of that journey was, we do not know, but obviously Turner
and Abbott were by now acquainted. Abbott becomes a freeman in December 1780
as a preparation for trading in London; and in 1781 occurs the earliest mention of
the partnership, in *Bailey's Northern Directory*:

Turner & Abbott, Staffordshire-potters china and glass men, 9, Old Fish Street in
London.[7]

Probably the glass business was a sideline of Abbott's. In a letter to Hannah
Abbott, dated 1814, from her Uncle John in New Jersey, mention is made of 'John
& Samuel Moss, Merchants in Philadelphia . . . now in the greatest respectability
of Merchants . . . one of them was formerly a glass engraver and worked for my
dear Brother'. A doggerel self-portrait in Abbott's handwriting contains these lines:

> Whilst time flew on swiftly, (he) would not let his time pass,
> Without learning some Art, or improving flint Glass,
> The latter to such great perfection he brought,
> As exceeds all descript'on, as well as all thought.

In 1782 Turner and Abbott moved their business from Old Fish Street to 81
Fleet Street, at the corner of St Bride's Passage. Among the Abbott Papers is a

broadsheet appeal for the upkeep of St Bride's spire. An engraving at the top of the sheet shows the church flanked by glass-fronted shops. That on the right was the premises of Turner and Abbott, consisting of a shop, warehouse, and rooms where pottery was gilded and enamelled, and glass engraved. Above these were apartments in which Abbott and his family lived for a time. Their second daughter, Hannah, was born there in 1788. By 1783 the partners had taken over 82 Fleet Street as their main showroom.

Pasted into the front of *The Potter's Art* (*Lardner's Museum of Science No. 19*), a small anonymous book in the William Salt Library, Stafford, is the following advertisement, cut from an unknown newspaper, on which someone has written the date 1783:

STAFFORDSHIRE WARE

It was generally believed, for several Years, that there was only one Warehouse in London where the Public could be served with Staffordshire Ware of the first composition, and that would wear well, but since TURNER and ABBOTT have opened their Warehouse, No. 82, Fleet-street, the corner of Salisbury-square, it has been acknowledged by the Nobility and others of our own kingdom, Aussi bien comme les Princes & la Noblesse etranger, that their Ware in general is not only equal, but many articles much superior to any made; and having lately compleated some new dinner and desert-services, tea and coffee equipages, and a variety of other matchless things, the Proprietors flatter themselves that their assortment is now the most extensive of any in London, as all ranks of people may furnish their town and country houses, dairies, hunting seats, and cottages, with ware suitable for each place, and on reasonable terms.—They gratefully acknowledge the many obligations they are under to the Nobility and Public in general, both for their own favours and kind recommendations, and beg leave to assure them that nothing in their power shall be wanting to merit a continuance of it. Any kind of Staffordshire ware made to pattern, and neatly enamelled with cyphers, crests, coats of arms, or any other device. To remove the inconvenience of being in the public Warehouse, a large commodious room is fitted up to show the patterns.

N.B. A stock is always kept sufficient to supply the Merchants with two or three hundred hogsheads of Ware at a very short notice, and on the most advantageous terms.

The next mention of the partnership is in *Bailey's Western Directory* of 1784: 'Turner and Abbott, Potters to the Prince of Wales.'

All of George IV's accounts and private papers were burnt after his death. The quite innocent were destroyed with the quite scandalous. So there is no official record of the appointment of Turner and Abbott. William Turner, F.S.A., in *The Collector* (1907), refers to some chairs at Windsor Castle ornamented with Turner medallions. But no such chairs exist at Windsor today, neither is there any Turner ware at the Brighton Pavilion or in the palaces.

In 1784 Abbott married Elizabeth (Betty) Carter, daughter of John Carter, a Bridport currier, and his wife Hannah, daughter of Joshua Colfox (1681–1744), a clothier. Betty was then twenty-nine. They had one son, John, who according to his father was 'not quite correct in his intellects' and was sent to live with Andrew's sister Elizabeth, who had married, late in life, a Bradford Abbas man named Sherring, and had no children of her own. Andrew also had two daughters. One of them, Eliza, married a wealthy man named Michael Miller, and, according to John Abbott, had 'tender offspring'. The other, Hannah (1788–1873), married William Colfox in 1821. Her descendants have inherited a silhouette portrait of Andrew, a creamware pattern book, some Turner pottery, other relics, and the Abbott Papers, which have been lodged in the Dorset Record Office, together with the Colfox Papers, through the generosity of Sir Philip Colfox, the present head of the family.

Mr Donald Towner has kindly given me a copy of *The Morning Herald and Daily Advertiser* of 31 January, 1785, which contains the following advertisement:

> Turner and Abbot, Potters to his Royal Highness the Prince of Wales, and Manufacturers of Queen's, and all other sorts of Staffordshire Ware, No. 82 Fleet-street, have the honor to acquaint the Nobility and Public in general, that since they have established a Manufactory in London, for enamelling their goods, they are enabled, and will engage to finish a service of Ware to any Pattern, in the course of three or four days after the order is given, either with Crests, Cyphers, or Borders. They also flatter themselves that the great variety of table services, desert setts, dejeunés, and other things, which they have lately finished, and are now ready for sale, far exceeds that of any other house in the kingdom. Any single piece, or part of a service may be had separately, or broken services made up to any pattern. They likewise manufacture a very general assortment of Egyptian Black, and Bamboo, or Cane Colour Tea-pots, some elegantly mounted with silver spouts and chains, and Mugs and Jugs, with silver rims and covers; also Mortars and Pestles of so hard a composition, that the strongest acids cannot penetrate them, are much more durable than marble, and not subject as those are, to wear away, and intermix with whatever is pounded in them, consequently far preferable either for the Chemist, Apothecary, or Kitchen. Such Ladies, Gentlemen, Merchants, and others, as may be pleased to honor the proprietors with their favours, may rest assured of having them executed in the best manner, and on the most reasonable terms. N.B.—Their Warehouse and Show-room are kept agreeably warm.

The creamware plate illustrated in Plate 27b is an example of Turner's crested ware. It is enamelled with the crest of the Rasdall family (two arms embowed in armour holding in hand proper a human heart gules enflamed proper charged with a tower argent).

In 1766 Wedgwood had written to his partner:

> Crests are very bad things for us (Potters) to meddle with & I never take any orders for services so ornamented. Plain ware if it sho^d not happen to be firsts, you will take off my hands as seconds, which if crested wo^d be useless as most other Crests, & Crest wearers are, for this & other reasons, the additional expence is more than the buyer can be perswaded to believe it ought to be.[8]

Wedgwood suggested that Sadler of Liverpool might crest ware for Bentley. But when Turner and Abbott opened their rooms in London, Wedgwood sent his wares there to be crested for his customers. The enamelling on the services made for Viscount Courtenay's daughters and their husbands by Wedgwood (in 1778) and Turner (in 1788) is obviously by the same hand. 'Was this outside decorator "Abbot" of 82 Fleet Street?' asks Mr Donald Towner in the *Transactions* of the English Ceramic Circle. Almost certainly he was, or, to be more precise, an employee in the Turner-Abbott *atelier*. In 1793 Joseph Lygo, the London representative of the Derby factory, wrote to William Duesbury that Abbott and Newbury put crests on foreign china.[9]

In the Fleet Street showrooms customers would be invited to thumb through pattern books like that now in the possession of Mrs Constance Hare (*née* Colfox), a descendant of Andrew Abbott. The book, bound in red leather, contains twenty-eight patterns, painted in water-colour on watermarked Whatman paper. Of these, the first twenty-two are borders, for use on plates and other wares (Plate 29a). Mr A. T. Morley Hewitt possesses an unmarked creamware frog mug, probably made by Turner, painted with border 26 (Plates 30 and 31). The last five designs are for whole plates (Plate 29b). The book is inscribed, inside the front cover, 'Miss Abbott. February 6th 1808'. She was evidently given the book by her father when its usefulness to him was over. At the back of the book are passages copied by her from improving works—'The Beauty and Advantages of Morning Exercise', 'A Receipt for Composing a Modern Love Letter', and other moral fragments.

Another thing which we learn from the *Morning Herald* advertisement is that some Turner wares were sold already mounted in silver. For example, the silver rim of the mug illustrated in Plate 15 bears the London date-mark for 1794. Here again, Wedgwood had the first word. In 1768 he wrote to Bentley:

> Mr Boulton is picking up Vases, & going to make them in Bronze. You know how old China bowles, Jarrs &c are mounted in Metal, he proposes an alliance betwixt the Pottery & Metal branches, Viz, that we shall make such things as will be suitable for

mounting & not have a *Pott* look, & he will finish them with the mounts. . . . We can make things for mounting with great facility, & dispatch, & mount^g will enhance their value greatly in the eye of the *purchacers*. Pebble in particular will in this way scarcely be discover'd to be counterfeit. Bass reliefs will have a most fine effect too, & will fetch *Guineas* instead of *shillings*. These things will do for the East India Co. & they give any price for *fine things*, 20 or £30,000 a piece for Clocks I am told is a common price with them to give.[10]

Among the Abbott Papers is a draft for a newspaper advertisement in Abbott's handwriting, undated, but probably roughly contemporary with the *Morning Herald* advertisement of 1785:

Turner and Abbott, Potters to His Royal Highness the Prince of Wales, No 82 Fleet Street, have the honour to acquaint the Nobility and Publick in general, that they have completed a variety of elegant and superb articles for Tea and Coffee services, Dejeunes, &c. made of the hardest and most perfect porcelain composition in the world, the ground or body is of a fine rich blue that will bear a Polish equal to any precious stones, the ornaments are groups of Figures, Beasts, Birds, Insects, &c in Bas. Rel. exquisitely modeled and of a delicate and incomparable whiteness. The proprietors have also added many capital hands to their Manufactory in Town for enamelling their Queen's ware and other goods, whereby they are enabled, in the course of a few days, to finish in the most masterly stile, any number of Table and Dessert Services, either with coats of arms, crests, cyphers or borders, of any pattern or colour. Their Mortars and Pestles which resist the most corrosive acids, are far superior to marble or Metal ones, as they do not (like these) corrode or intermix with whatever is Levigated in them, consequently they are far preferable either for the chemist, Apothecary or Family use. Captains and others going to the East Indies will find here a more general assortm^t of goods properly adapted for that Country than at any other house in the Kingdom—with this singular advantage, that they may have new Patterns done to their own fancy at a very short notice for every voyage. They also keep a very large general assortment of plain Queen's ware for common use, together with a matchless variety of Hunting Jugs and Mugs some mounted with Silver—and Teapots mounted with Silver spouts and chains.

The reference to officers of the East India Company is particularly interesting, for among the Abbott Papers is a bond dated 16 December 1786, stating that Charles Henry Stone, second officer to the East India Company's ship *Princess Royal* is bound to J. Turner and Andrew Abbott of Fleet Street in the City of London, merchants, in the penal sum of £227. 9s. A similar document of 29 February 1788 binds Robert Beard, captain's cook of the East India Company's vessel *Triton* to William Turner, Andrew Abbott, and J. Benjamin Newbury in the sum of £63. 16s. And on 28 March 1789, John Bromley, purser of the ship *Earl of Oxford*, was bound to the same partnership in the sum of £94. 6s.

In 1787 Joseph Lygo wrote to William Duesbury of Derby that 'Turner and Abbott, Staffordshire potters' had tried to see the clockmaker Vulliamy, with the object of superseding Duesbury as supplier of the biscuit figures with which Vulliamy decorated his clocks. The workbooks of Vulliamy, preserved at the British Horological Institute, show that in the period 1797–1806 Duesbury continued to supply the clockmaker with biscuit figures, and that Wedgwood sold him jasper medallions, but there is no mention of Turner and Abbott.

On 21 December 1787 John Turner I died. He was buried in a handsome sarcophagus in Brewood churchyard, with others of his family. The *Gentleman's Magazine* noted in its obituary column:

24 [*sic*] (December) Mr Turner, partner with Mr Abbott, potter, Fleet-Street.[11]

In his will[12] Turner left £1,500 to each of his three daughters, and divided the potworks and other property between his sons—three-fifths to William, two-fifths to John. Provision was made for several workmen, including an annuity of 6s. for Joseph Booth. Turner's servant, Elizabeth Slinn, received £10. William Turner was now 25, his brother, 21. Together they ran the Staffordshire business and maintained the partnership with Abbott.

The Abbott Papers include the London account book of the partnership for the years 1788–94. These accounts, which are admirably clear, enable us to trace the fortunes of the partnership in some detail. It seems to have been a period of considerable prosperity for the firm. Sales rose by 32 per cent, from an annual average of £11,000 in 1788 and the first half of 1789 to £14,500 in the year ending in August 1793, although, with the outbreak of war against France, they fell back to £11,500 in the following year. We do not know enough about the London pottery market in this period to be able to judge how far, if at all, this increase in sales was achieved at the expense of competitors. But we do know that the period covered by the accounts was one of very rapid economic growth in the country as a whole— Professor Rostow regards the years 1783–1802 as the 'take-off' period in British economic history[13]—and one would have expected the increasing pace of economic activity to be reflected in a sharp rise in the demand for luxury goods of all sorts.

The rise in net profits, although somewhat less steady, was even greater than the rise in sales. They rose by almost a third between 1789 and 1792, from £1,700 to £2,500, and after a sharp decline in 1793, attributable apparently to an increase in stocks and a substantial rise in selling costs, they reached a new peak of £2,600 in 1794. Over the period as a whole, apart from 1792–3, there was a steady improvement in profit margins. Net profits as a percentage of total sales rose from just under 15 per cent in 1788–9 to about 19 per cent in 1791–2 and 22 per cent in 1793–4. There was also a slight improvement in the return on capital employed.

There is no doubt that the Turners did well out of the partnership. Yet there are indications in the accounts that all may not have been well. From the outset they were drawing heavily on their capital. Between February 1788 and August 1789 they withdrew £2,200 from the business. In March 1789 they borrowed £1,500 from James Maidment[14] on security of their share in the partnership. This was duly repaid in 1791 from their own holding. Finally, in August 1792 they sold out altogether. During the same period the other partners, Abbott and Newbury,[15] were ploughing back a substantial proportion of their share of the profits, and even, on occasions, adding to their original holding from outside the partnership. In February 1788 the Turners' share in the partnership was almost three-fifths; by the time of their final withdrawal in 1792 it had fallen to substantially less than a third. Twice, then, they seem to have been in difficulties: in the period 1788–9, and again in 1792. These are roughly the dates when the sources suggest they were in trouble. In 1789 the French were withholding payment of debts, while 1792 is the most likely year for William Turner's imprisonment.

Abbott's descendants had a different explanation for the Turners' decline. In 1868 Hannah Colfox, then 80, told her grandchildren that she 'remembered her father saying his partner Wm Turner lived in Staffordshire, they were partners in a China trade, Mr Abbott residing at the Warehouse in Fleet Street. This Turner was the maker of the Jasper Ware marked with his name, she heard he was of very extravagant habits and dissipated his means.'

Speaking of the Turner ware then in her possession, Hannah Colfox said: 'The beads and knife handles were considered failures as a matter of trade.' The many vases and other ornaments in her possession had been selected by Andrew Abbott for his house in Clapham. 'Coffee cups and saucers were sold at £1. 1. 0 each. Jasper vases 11¼" high at £3. 3. 0 each and 10" at £2. .2. 0. The vases with rich bas relief were much more expensive. The subject called "the infant academy", a cupid artist and sitter, is taken from Sir Joshua Reynolds.'

After their withdrawal from the partnership the Turners maintained business relations with Abbott and Newbury. They must have had a 'sale or return' arrangement, for an entry of 26 May 1795 in Abbott's account book reads:

> Messrs W. & J. Turner.
> To Jasper not pay till sold. 7-13-0.

On 16 August 1802 Abbott and Newbury paid the Turners £44. 4s. 2d. in full settlement. It is of more than incidental interest that, on the same date, J. Spode was paid £54. R. Baddeley £59. 0s. 9d., and Wood and Caldwell £25. 3s., all in full settlement. For all these potters are known to have had some association with John Turner I—with the exception of Enoch Wood, and even he is claimed by one writer,[16] though on no stated authority, as having been one of Turner's modellers. Josiah Spode had been with Turner at Stoke in 1756. Ralph Baddeley was involved in the leasing of Shelton Hall to Turner in 1779,[17] and may have known him earlier, at Daniel Bird's factory.[18] James Caldwell, Recorder of Newcastle-under-Lyme, was a witness to his will in 1785, and, incidentally, lived at Stoneyfields, King Street, the house now occupied by Mrs Young.

These settlements were a prelude to the dissolution of the Abbott-Newbury partnership by a deed of 14 October 1802. Abbott now became a partner of James Underhill Mist. Preserved with the Abbott Papers is a copper plate for printing billheads. At the top of the left-hand side is an engraving of the Prince of Wales's feathers, and beneath it is the inscription:

London . . . 18 . . .

B*ot* of Abbott & Mist, Potters to his Royal Highness the Prince of Wales. Their Manufacture is sold at their Warehouse No. 82 Fleet Street, together with all sorts of china and glass and where they have a manufactory for gilding their wares with coats of arms, crests, cyphers, Borders, or any other Device.

Account books show that the partnerships, between 1801 and 1808, decorated and sold ware for the following potters:

Airey Cookson & Co.	John Mare
J. & E. Baddeley	Miles Mason
Zachariah Barnes	Minton Poulstong [Poulson] & Co.
Arthur Burrow	Jane Moss
Chetham & Woolley	Newell & Cotton
Coltman & Co.	W. H. Price
Coomer & Co.	Rhead & Goodfellow
J. Davenport	John & Geo. Rogers
G. & J. Egginton	Rose & Co.
Forrester & Mayer	Thos. Ryland
Charles Harvey	James Smith & Co.
J. & G. Hawkes	J. Troby
John Heath	Turners Glover & Co.
Hollins, Warburton & Co.	David Wilson
J. & W. Holmes	Robt. Wilson

The partnership was dissolved in 1811, when Abbott, now 68, retired from business. Mist continued at the Fleet Street premises, which he had leased from Abbott in 1810 for 10½ years less two days.

To say that Mist is a somewhat nebulous figure is to express the unhappy truth in an unhappy pun. We know nothing of his antecedents. He seems to have stood in relation to Abbott rather as John Voyez did to Wedgwood: a Chaucerian rogue, whose alleged crimes seem less heinous than comic in retrospect. One of his first actions after the break with Abbott was to give Abbott's clerk, Trais, notice to leave. In these circumstances, Trais's view of Mist was probably jaundiced, but his letter to Abbott of 7 June 1812 gives some idea of Mist's character:

> Mr Mist's very obliging Disposition to his Customers I have heard of at this place. A Lady of this town came to his house with an order for him but thro' his Politeness to her she took it away again to a Nother House. He has very little to Do, and when he sells a Table Sett he has it all Brought to the Front of the Door and on Direction Putt on it to lett all the World Know as they Pass by, What a Deal of Business his Done; you had no occasion when you was in Business to Do the like.

Trais evidently thought that his complaints were falling on sympathetic ears, and it certainly seems likely, from a letter written by Abbott to an unknown friend on 2 November 1811, that the Abbott-Mist partnership had not been a pattern of harmony:

> I assure you it would give me great pleasure if any suggestion of mine could in the least contribute to afford you that assistance & relief which you stand so much in need of;—I know but of three ways by which to accomplish so desirable an end; the first is partnership, but past experience forbids me to recommend that on any account whatsoever. . . .

Possibly Abbott was also referring in this letter to his partnership with the Turners. We recall his opinion, relayed by his daughter, that William Turner was 'of very extravagant habits and dissipated his means'.

The Turners continued to sell ware through Mist. A willow-pattern plate in my possession (Plate 24b) bears the impressed mark

TURNER
MIST SOLE AGENT.

Mr and Mrs J. K. des Fontaines have in their collection a thistle-shaped vase (Plate 25a) impressed

J. MIST, 82
FLEET STREET
LONDON.

It may be that these marks were used to indicate two different classes of wares: those which were sold for Turner by Mist at a percentage commission, and those which the Turners made for Mist, to be sold at his own price. But, in fact, the des Fontaines vase seems too coarse and unfinished to be a Turner piece, and may have been made by an inferior potter, like Holland, Keeling, or Shorthose.

The final settlement of account between Mist and Abbott was protracted until 1814 by outstanding debts and by Mist's dishonesty. Lord O'Neil, one of their chief debtors, absconded first to Ireland, and later to France. Other debts were owed by Members of Parliament, and Abbott complains, 'It is a great hardship upon tradesmen that the priviledge [*sic*] of Parliament sh[ld] be so much abused, & that any of its members sh[d] shelter themselves under it, & not pay their just debts.' Another complication was the non-delivery of two crates of Turner wares.[19]

In considering the dishonesty of Mist, we must remember that only one side of the story is presented by the Abbott Papers. Counsel for the defence are lacking. On the other hand, the chief witness for the prosecution is a reliable one: Abbott emerges from the correspondence as a man of rigid integrity. His righteous indignation, which seems perhaps a little high-handed to a more dispassionate age, was then the predictable reaction of a peppery Unitarian moralist. The substance of Abbott's allegations is that Mist was deceiving him as to which debts he had received. For example, Mist received a debt of £262. 14s.s 10d. from a Mr John Pickersgill in Russia. He failed to enter it in the books of the late joint account, and, though he wrote to Abbott in the next few days, did not mention the receipt of this and other monies. Mist, for his part, accused Trais of collecting debts to which the late partners were entitled. The Abbott correspondence tails off after 1814, so we do not know the final outcome of these disputes. In November 1814 Abbott instructed his solicitors, Messrs Anstice and Cox, to take legal action against Mist. Probably this had the desired effect.

In 1818 Abbott leased the Fleet Street premises to Messrs J. & J. Davenport for ten years. In 1844 John Phelps and William and Hannah Colfox re-leased the premises to Messrs Davenport for fourteen years. In 1858 Phelps and Mrs Colfox leased it to William Davenport for a further fourteen years. No. 15 of Tallis's *London Street Views* (1838) shows 82 Fleet Street under the Davenport régime. In the Guildhall Museum is a similar view by James Findlay, a tinted drawing of about 1845 (Plate 25b). Although the numbering of Fleet Street has been changed since the eighteenth century—it now runs in the opposite direction—No. 82 still stands on the site of Turner's showroom, at the entrance to Salisbury Court. The Westminster Bank (now 82 and 83 Fleet Street) covers the precise area formerly occupied by the various partnerships. The original buildings of 81 and 82 Fleet Street were demolished when the street was widened in the nineteenth century. Compensation was paid to the Colfox family, and with it most of the land now owned by Sir Philip Colfox at Symondsbury, Dorset, was bought.

Abbott lived until 1819. In 1811 he had moved house from Clapham. The household effects and 'a few lots of old fine old port' were sold on the premises, near the corner of Acre Lane, on 24 June. He and his wife settled at 64 St Thomas Street, Weymouth. Mrs Abbott, who had been an invalid for some years, died at Weymouth in 1815, and was buried near her mother in her native town of Bridport.

In the following year Abbott moved to Bridport because there was no Unitarian chapel at Weymouth. He confided to his brother-in-law that 'my pace is with increasing age becoming more like that of the snail than the deer'. He was also going deaf, and for the last two years of his life was completely blind. When no longer able to take walks he took the air in a sedan chair.

Although he can have received little formal education, Abbott was a voracious reader. His surviving manuscript books show that in 1774–5 he was studying astronomy, mathematics, and Cronstadt's *System of Minerology and Natural Philosophy*. He later made use of his knowledge of mineralogy in analysing samples of clay and stones from Seatown to find out whether they would be of use in making china. He owned a third edition of the *Encyclopaedia Britannica*, which was housed in the fine bookcase now at Symondsbury Manor, which Abbott had made by Jenks, the London cabinet-maker, in 1811, to his own specifications. He was an enthusiastic poetaster. Apart from the manuscript self-portrait already mentioned, there survives a printed acrostic, crude both in prosody and sentiment, on Bonaparte—

THE COMPOSITION AND CHARACTER

OF THE

FIRST CONSUL.

ACROSTIC EXTEMPORE, BY A. A. FLEET STREET.

B LOWN by the Blast from *Satan's* hottest Fire,
O n Earth his Minister, Priest, and Liar;
N ature's foul Excrement of hellish Brood,
A Villain ripe for Cruelty and Blood,
P uff'd up with Pride, a Stranger to all good;
A Friend to none, an Enemy to all,
R eady to murder, where his Vengeance fall.
T o rid the World of such a Monster, hail!
E ach Briton who shall first the Wretch assail.

Printed by Sabine & Son, Shoe Lane, London.

evidence, perhaps, that Abbott, and by implication the Turners, had suffered personally from the depredations of the First Consul.

Even when completely blind, Abbott was still active. 'James also informed us', wrote John Abbott from Philadelphia in October 1818, 'that my dear afflicted brother amus'd himself in working at the Cooper's trade, and that he kept his tools in a glass case on his mantelpiece—very strange if true.'

Abbott died in 1819 in a house on the corner of Magdalen Lane, Westallington, Bridport, and was buried in the graveyard of the Unitarian chapel. The Abbott Papers include the bill for the funeral expenses, and Mrs Constance Hare possesses the *memento mori*, a ring whose bezel contains a plaited lock of his hair under glass, with the interlaced initials 'AA' superimposed. In his will, made on 1 April 1819, and proved in London on 10 November 1819, Abbott left £2,000 to his daughter Eliza Miller, and the Fleet Street premises to Hannah Abbott, later Colfox.

NOTES TO CHAPTER EIGHT

[1] M. H. Grant, *The Makers of Black Basaltes* (1910), p. 306.

[2] William Chaffers, *Hand-Book of Marks and Monograms* (1952 edn), p. 344.

[3] William Bacchus (*c.* 1783–7) is recorded in contemporary directories and surveys as a manufacturer of creamwares. Mankowitz and Haggar (p. 12) suggest that the Thomas Bacchus referred to by Shaw as marrying a widow named Astbury, and as making cream-coloured and blue-painted earthenware, may be an erroneous reference to William Bacchus.

[4] Apsley Pellatt, or Pellat, of the Falcon Glass House, Southwark, took out a patent for cameo glass in 1819. The Green of Thames Street must surely have been an ancestor of that James Green who was trading from Upper Thames Street in the nineteenth century, and who acted as English agent to the Limoges factory.

[5] MS. 4337/5, Guildhall Library, London.

[6] Josiah Spode I, for example, was admitted to the Freedom of the City of London as a Liveryman of the Spectacle Makers' Company; his certificate of admission, dated 16 June 1778, is illustrated opposite p. 16 of Arthur Hayden's *Spode and His Successors* (1925).

[7] John Turner had been trading from this address on his own since at least 1775, for in that year his name was included in *The London Register of Merchants and Traders*, printed by W. Harris: 'Turner John, potter, 9 Old Fish-Street.'

'Old Fish Street ran east and west parallel to Cheapside from Queen Victoria Street to Knightrider Street; it is now called Knightrider Street.' (Eilert Ekwall, *Street-Names of the City of London*, 1954, p. 74.)

The *Morning Herald* of 8 July 1786 advertised the sale by auction of the stock in trade of Mr Clark Durnford, 'China Glass and Staffordshire Warehouseman', 'on the premises, in Little Knight, Rider Street, Doctor's Commons'. Possibly Durnford took over the premises vacated by Turner and Abbott.

[8] Josiah Wedgwood to Thomas Bentley, 25 September 1766. (*Letters of Josiah Wedgwood 1762–72*, ed. Lady Farrer, p. 103.)

[9] Quoted F. Brayshaw Gilhespy, 'Joseph Lygo's Letters to Derby', E.C.C. *Transactions*, vol iii, part v, p. 208.

[10] Josiah Wedgwood to Thomas Bentley, 21 November 1768. (*Letters of Josiah Wedgwood, 1762–72*, ed. Lady Farrer, p. 233.)

[11] *Gentleman's Magazine*, December 1787, p. 1196.

[12] Drawn up 14 September 1785, proved 12 October 1789.

[13] W. W. Rostow, *The Stages of Economic Growth* (1960) p. 9.

[14] James Maidment was the partner of James Neale of Staffordshire and St Paul's Churchyard, who, like John Turner, had married a Brewood girl. It is just possible that Maidment, like Abbott, came of a Dorset, even a Bradford Abbas, family. When John Chiles and Margaret Hurt were married at Bradford Abbas on 30 December 1783 one of the witnesses was a John Maidment. (Bradford Abbas parish register, Dorset Record Office.)

[15] J. Benjamin Newbury (Newberry, Newbery) was the Turners' and Abbott's partner. On 25 October 1807, John Newberry of Arrow Court, Fleet Street, was buried at St Dunstan's in the West, Fleet Street. This may well have been the same man, but in any event the Newbury family had a long connexion with Fleet Street and its neighbourhood. From the bookseller Ralph Newbery of Fleet Street, who issued books between 1560 and his death in 1633, was descended John Newbery (1713–67) of St Paul's Churchyard, publisher of children's books. John Newbery was a friend of Dr Johnson and Oliver Goldsmith, who wrote for him. He also sold the famous Dr James's Fever Powder, and his son Francis inherited this side of the business. (Charles Welsh, *A Bookseller of the Last Century*, 1885; F. J. Harvey Darton, *Children's Books in England*, 1932, ch. viii.)

[16] 'It is supposed that Enoch Wood served under him [John Turner I] as a modeller.' (William Turner, *The Collector*, 1907, p. 44.)

[17] G. E. Stringer, *New Hall Porcelain* (1949), p. 11.

[18] That there was at some time a connexion between Ralph Baddeley and Daniel Bird is suggested by the name the former chose for his son—Daniel Bird Baddeley. (*Victoria History of Staffordshire*, viii, 153; and White's *History, Gazeteer and Directory of Staffordshire*, 1834, p. 559.) Ralph Baddeley had married Sarah Bird at Stoke on 1 February 1772.

[19] On 8 January 1813, Mist wrote to Abbott:

'. . . I will give you £38. 3 which is the difference in your favour & will close our account of Capital—& will myself pay Pickford & Pellett & from the sums due to them, provided you will write to Mr Neal & get the Crates of Turner deliver to me; and allow me the proceeds of all debts due to us, further being understood I am not to be charged for that Crate of twiflers ££—which in amount was but small after Coverage of the large qunt. broke is deduct'd.'

Abbott accordingly wrote to Neale, from Weymouth (19 January 1813):

'Sir, Yesterday's post brought me a letter from Mr Mist saying he had received from Mr W. Turner only one Crate out of the three, of those settled for, at your house, which you engaged should all be delivered without delay, being the approp. conditions at the time of settlement, the two Crates deficient amount to nearly Thirty pounds, therefore beg you will immediately enquire the reason why these goods have not been sent, & get them delivered to Mr Mist as soon as possible, as I have no doubt but you will consider yourself in Justice and Honour bound to do it & I remain Sir yours respectfully.

Your ansr. to Mr. Mist on the subject will be sufficient.'

On 2 February, Abbott wrote to Mist, telling him the contents of his letter to Neale, and recommending him to call on Neale if he did not hear from him, to ascertain whether Neale would have the crates delivered or not. On 8 February, Mist replied:

'I have not had any information respectg. the Crates from Turners in consequence of your letter to Mr Neal, have now sent to him & conclude this month his Reply

'Mr. Neal informs me he has sent your letter to Wm Turner requesting the delivy. of said goods; but myself knowing he is not in a situation to return or to do anything I never expect they will be delivd.'

Abbott wrote back, on 10 February:

'Yours of the 8th is now before me, as to Turners Crates, Mr Neale at the settling the account before two witnesses, pledged himself that he would be accountable for the delivery of the Crates, therefore he is in honour and Justice bound to do it.'

As this is the last reference to the Turner crates in the correspondence, we do not know whether they were eventually delivered, or whether the Turners were in such straits at this time that they were unable to honour their obligations.

CHAPTER NINE

The End of the Factory

FROM 1795 ONWARDS we can trace the activities of the Turners in the files of the *Staffordshire Advertiser*, a weekly paper founded in that year. William Turner, not surprisingly, considering his experiences in France, joined the Volunteers. On 11 October 1798, as a captain, he commanded the Lane End Volunteers at a Grand Field Day on the Brampton, Newcastle-under-Lyme.[1] By 1800 he had been promoted to major, and on 18 September his wife, with Miss Gresley, the sister of Sir Nigel Gresley, presented regimental colours to the Lane End Volunteers.[2] The corps was assembled on a piece of ground 'near Sir John Heathcote's at Longton'.[3] Major Turner, as commandant, made a short speech—his only recorded utterance. 'Be assured,' he said, 'that this Standard, presented by the hand of Female Worth and Excellence, will be considered doubly valuable.'[4] The corps he had the honour to command would preserve and defend it 'to the latest period of their lives'.[5] The ladies who presented the colours were richly dressed in the uniform of the corps. Sir John Heathcote, who acted as reviewing officer, 'gave an elegant dejeuné at his house at Longton to the Trentham troop of Yeomanry, and officers of other corps; and a sumptuous dinner was given by Cornet S. Spode. The various corps of Volunteers were regaled at the different inns in Lane End. The manoeuvres were performed in a masterly stile, and the day being favourable upwards of 10,000 spectators assembled.'[6] A Turner mould, preserved at the Spode-Copeland factory museum, shows a master potter, with cravat, wig, and gaiters, throwing a pot while an apprentice turns the throwing-wheel. The master's rifle rests against his chair, with his plumed hat hanging from the muzzle: he is a Volunteer.

Ward, in his *History of Stoke-on-Trent*, writes:

> On the renewal of the war with France in 1803, when more vigorous measures for the invasion of England were made by Napoleon, half a million men came forward as volunteers—the Hanley and Shelton volunteers were commanded by Liet-Col. James Whitehead: the Lane End volunteers mustered four companies and were commanded by Major William Turner.[7]

On 9 October 1799 William Turner had married, at St Mary's Church, Stafford,

Elizabeth Wright, the eldest daughter of John Wright, a Stafford banker.[8] His brother married, on 23 November 1803, Mary Hyde, the second daughter of Nathaniel Hyde of Ardwick Green, Manchester.[9] John Turner was living the life of a country gentleman at Lightwood Lodge, about a mile from Lane End. The *Staffordshire Advertiser* records the granting to him of game certificates in 1795,[10] 1797,[11] and 1801.[12] William Turner owned a farm at Weston Coyney in the parish of Caverswall.

In 1803 the Turners formed a partnership with John Glover and Charles Simpson. Glover was their brother-in-law: he had married Sarah Turner at Trentham on 10 August 1801.[13] Simpson had been confidential clerk to John Turner I, and was a witness to his will on 14 September 1785. He was born in 1754, the third son of Isaac and Mary Simpson of Wolstanton, and was baptized there on 23 June.[14] On 28 May 1793 he married, at St Giles's Church, Newcastle-under-Lyme, Mrs Sarah Clive, a widow for whom the Heathcotes of Longton Hall, with whom she was friendly, had obtained a house at Lane End.

On 10 November 1804 John Turner withdrew from the partnership.[15] The witness to his retirement was Broadhurst Harding, the owner of the Gerverot beaker. John Turner became manager at the factory of Minton, Poulson, and Pownall at Stoke, where 'he effected great improvements in the bodies and glazes and in the general character of the productions of the works'.[16]

On 20 and 21 November the Weston Coyney farming stock and household furniture of William Turner was sold by auction.[17] On 27 March 1806 the partnership of Turner, Glover, and Simpson was dissolved.[18] A separate declaration announced that the manufacture would be carried on by William Turner.[19] Glover took over the cart and carrying business of Thomas Colclough at Stone.[20] Charles Simpson, with his wife and her son, John Henry Clive, remained at Lane End until 1809, when they moved to Newfield, Tunstall, and worked the potteries at Sandyford, then vacated by the Cartlich family. Simpson died at Newfield Hall on 11 November 1827.[21] His widow went to live with her son at Chell House, Wolstanton. She died there on 3 June 1833, aged 84,[22] and was buried beside Simpson in the churchyard of St James, Newchapel.

In the *Staffordshire Advertiser* of 12 April 1806 it was announced that a sale would be held on 14 April at the Manufactory of Messrs Turner, Glover, and Simpson, at Lane End', of:

> Fifty tons of Blue Clay, thirty tons of Black Clay, thirty tons of Cracking Clay, upwards of three thousand pecks of Flint, five tons of Composition, five Printing Presses, old Cylinders, and a quantity of old Iron.

And also four capital draught Horses, gearing for four horses, a waggon, six carts, and various other articles.

On 19 April a notice in the *Staffordshire Advertiser* postponed this sale to the 25th. In the same issue of 19 April another advertisement appeared which, as it describes the Turner potbank in some detail, is worth quoting in full:

MOST ELIGIBLE SET OF POTWORKS
TO BE LET
For a Term of 12 Years, from 11th of May next.

An old established and well accustomed Manufactory, lately occupied by Messrs Turner & Co. at Lane End, in the Staffordshire Potteries; where the making of Porcelain, & Earthenware, in all its branches, has been carried on to a great extent, for a great number of years. The Manufactory embraces advantages, seldom or ever to be met with in similar situations, in affording a never failing supply of water, and the ready delivery of Coals, by a Railway, within 40 yards of the Pit's Mouth; even without the assistance of a Horse. This singular advantage in a consumption of 40 Tons of Coal per week, would render a direct saving of £150 per Annum. And as a Railway is now laid from Lane End to Stoke, the necessity of keeping a team of horses for this Manufactory will be completely obviated.

The Works comprize every necessary appendage for carrying on a Porcelain and Earthenware Manufactory to a great extent. The Warehouses are excellently fitted up on the most approved plan, and the whole in good repair.

The Works are excellently furnished with all Implements, Fixtures &c. necessary for immediate beginning to work.

All Implements, Fixtures, &c. to be taken at a valuation.

Refer to Mr. CHARLES SIMPSON, at Lane End, who will give every information.

The word 'porcelain' can probably be here taken as referring to the 'Turner's Patent' wares, not to any more refined form of china. The potworks were taken over by Richard Woolley, who had previously been in partnership with Ann Chetham at Lane End.[23]

On 5 July 1806 came the announcement of the bankruptcy of the Turner brothers.[24] On 20 August William Turner's farming stock and household furniture at Moorville were sold.[25] On 21 August the farming stock and furniture of John Turner was sold at Lightwood Lodge.[26] On 25 November a sale was held at the Union Hotel, Lane End, of:

FOUR pieces of LAND, situate at Lightwood, near Land End aforesaid, called the Little Crab Tree Leasow, Crab Tree Leasow, Schemers Meadow, and Old Ben's Meadow, containing together 22A. or 27P.

The abovementioned lands are part of Lightwood Farm, and held by lease under the Marquis of Stafford, for the lives of Mr William Turner, aged 44, and Mr John Turner, aged 41, and the life of the survivor.

For further particulars apply to Sir J. E. HEATHCOTE, at Longton Hall, or to Mr TOMLINSON, Solicitor, Hanley.[27]

On 16 June 1807 the sale began, at the Union Hotel, Lane End, of:

A Large and elegant assortment of Earthenware, and China; comprising the different articles usually manufactured, both useful and ornamental; and consisting of Cream Colour, China-glazed blue edge, china glaze printed and painted, Egyptian Black, Cane, Stone, Jasper, Pearl, and Patent China Goods; being the well known, and highly reputed manufacture of Messrs TURNER and Co. of Lane-end aforesaid; . . . The purchasers will also have an opportunity of matching, and continuing the patterns, at Mr WILLIAM TURNER'S present Manufactory, in Lane-End, and Merchants, Tradesmen, Commission packers, and others, will find their account in attending the above sale, which offers advantages of rare occurrence.[28]

William Turner's 'neat Household Furniture, Valuable Books, and other effects' were sold at his house in Lane End on 25 and 26 May 1813.[29] The books are of especial interest, as providing the originals of some of the Turners' designs. They consisted of:

Hamilton's Antiquities, 4 vols. Herculaneum and Etruscan Antiquities, 7 vols. Montfaucon's Antiquities, 5 vols. Plaw's Architecture; Italian Views; Botanical Magazine, 14 vols. Repertory of Arts, 18 vols. Bewick's Quadrupeds; Smith's Laboratory, 2 vols. Grew's Anatomy of Plants; Parles' Chemical Catechism; Sinclair's Account of Scotland, 4 vols. Society of Arts, 6 vols. Sturm's Reflections; Monro's Anatomy; Pergolesi's Engravings; Beceuil [*sic*], &c. Sculptures: and many other valuable Publications.[30]

The furniture and effects of Lightwood Lodge were sold up on 21 and 22 September 1815.[31] John Turner's library was rather less antiquarian than his brother's:

14 volumes of Bath Agriculture, 18 volumes of Racing Calendar, Sportsman's Dictionary, 7 volumes, Society of Arts, Description Pierre's Gravees, Crew's Anatomy of Plants, 2 volumes, Travels of Count Stotberg, 2 volumes of Johnson's Dictionary, Linnaeus' Animal Kingdom, &c. &c.[32]

His effects reveal the same catholicity of taste. They included 'a fowling piece, two bows and arrows, quantity of copper printing plates, side saddle, hack saddle and bridles'.[33] In July 1812, when he contributed £1. 1s. to the Branch Bible Society for Newcastle and the Potteries, John Turner was still living at Lane End. But subsequently he moved back to Brewood Hall, where he died on 26 June

1824.[34] A plaque in Brewood Church commemorates him and his wife, who died on 25 February 1840.

The end of the Turner factory came in 1829. On 12 December the following advertisement appeared in the *Pottery Mercury*:

EXCELLENT STOCK OF EARTHENWARE,
POTTERS' UTENSILS,
Copper-Plate Engravings, &c.
WILL BE SOLD BY AUCTION,
By MR JAMES,

Upon the Premises, at the manufactory, in High-street, Lane-End, on Monday, Tuesday, Wednesday, and Thursday, the 14th, 15th, 16th & 17th Days of December, 1829; the property of MR WILLIAM TURNER, who is declining the Potting Business;

THE FIXTURES and UTENSILS comprise One Biscuit Oven, excellent hardening-on kiln and Ovel [*sic*], with small kiln adjoining Marl house, 800 *Biscuit Saggars*, 800 *Glazed Saggars*, saggar bench and whirler, 7 saggar drums, 2 beating paddles, 2 maws, peg post, 80 Loads of piping, lot of turners' tools, excellent braze with a complete set of bits, 70 Saggar Shords, 520 workhouse boards, 4 *large saws*, *4 box door locks*, &c.

COPPER-PLATE ENGRAVINGS—1 Willow table service, complete, quite new; 1 table service complete, village pattern, with embossed block and working mould to match, all in excellent working condition; table service complete in 11 plates, sprig pattern, with block and working moulds to match; 1 tea set complete in 7 plates, bird pattern; 1 Brosely tea set complete in 10 plates; 1 wind-mill tea set complete in 8 plates; 1 tea set, temple pattern complete in 8 plates; 1 tea set, lady-day pattern complete in 6 plates; 1 jug set, shepherd pattern; 1 jug set, villager pattern; 1 ewer and bason set complete, villager pattern.

An excellent assortment of Block and working Moulds, all of excellent Shape and Modern Patterns.

THE EARTHENWARE will comprise about 4000 dozen of blue printed table and tea ware, 500 dozen of dipped and coloured ware, with a quantity of black teapots and cream ewers; ditto stone and ornaments, beautifully figured &c., all of which will be sold in lots to accommodate purchasers.—R. JAMES begs to state to purchasers that the ware is of the best quality, and all of excellent selling patterns.

The Utensils, Fixtures, and Engravings, will be Sold on Monday and Tuesday, the 14th and 15th inst., and the Earthenware on the two following Days.

N.B.—The Sale to commence each Day at One o'Clock.

Spode and Adams both bought quantities of the Turner moulds. Between 1881 and 1885 Messrs Gildea and Walker were still producing copies of Turner jasper wares. Jewitt, in 1878, said:

This consists of a terra-cotta body with a slip of various colours green, blue, chocolate, buff, etc., etc., decorated with bas-reliefs, many of which are Flaxman's designs, as used by Turner at his famous works of the last century, a large number of Turner's moulds belonging to the firm. The body, however, lacks the firmness, hardness and compact character of the old Turner ware.[35]

Messrs Gildea and Walker inherited the Turner moulds from their predecessors in the same factory. These included T. J. and J. Mayer (*c.* 1843–55), whose display at the 1851 Exhibition contained 'White stone-ware punch bowls, enamelled and gilt, and jugs with blue raised figures'. This firm was succeeded by Mayer Brothers & Elliot; Mayer and Elliot; Liddle, Elliot & Co.; Bates, Elliot & Co; Bates, Walker & Co; and Bates, Gildea & Walker. All these firms used the mark 'Turner Jasper Ware'. As for the Turner engravings, some were bought by Heathcote: in the Hanley Museum are a marked Heathcote plate and a marked Turner plate, with identical underglaze printing.

William Turner continued to live at Lane End, in what is now (1965) one of the worst slum areas in the Potteries—the street called Ashwood.[36] He died on 5 July 1835, 'one of the oldest manufacturers in the trade'.[37] Almost 60 years later, when the portrait of Elsie Maud Palmer—now Mrs Eric Young—was painted on a porcelain plaque by the Minton artist Anton Boullemier, her family had her described on the back as 'Great Grand daughter of Major Turner of Lane End', even though she was a more direct descendant of Humphrey Palmer of Hanley.

Elsie Maud
Daughter of Henry and Clara Palmer
Great Grand daughter of Major Turner
of Lane End.
painted by A. Boullemier.
1892.

NOTES TO CHAPTER NINE

[1] *Staffordshire Advertiser*, 13 October 1798.
[2] *Staffordshire Advertiser*, 27 September 1800.
[3] ibid.
[4] ibid.
[5] ibid.
[6] ibid.
[7] Ward, *History of Stoke-on-Trent* (1843), p. 59.
[8] Parish register, St Mary's Church, Stafford, and *Staffordshire Advertiser*, 12 October 1799.
[9] *Staffordshire Advertiser*, 26 November 1803.
[10] *Staffordshire Advertiser*, 29 August 1795.
[11] *Staffordshire Advertiser*, 16 September 1797.
[12] *Staffordshire Advertiser*, 5 September 1801.
[13] *Staffordshire Advertiser*, 10 August 1801.
[14] For the information about Charles Simpson and his wife in this chapter I am indebted to Percy W. L. Adams, *John Henry Clive (1781–1853) of North Staffordshire and his Descendants*, Newcastle-under-Lyme, 1947.
[15] *Staffordshire Advertiser*, 17 November 1804:

NOTICE IS HEREBY GIVEN

That the partnership between the undersigned William Turner, John Turner, John Glover, and Charles Simpson, manufacturers of porcelain and earthenware, at Lane End, in the Staffordshire Potteries, was this day dissolved by mutual consent, so far as regards the said John Turner, who has retired from the said concern. All persons indebted to the said late Copartnership, are to pay such debts to the said William Turner, John Glover, and Charles Simpson, who will discharge all just demands thereon: and by whom the said Manufactory will be carried on in future in all its various branches.

Dated this 10th day of November, 1804. WM. TURNER,
JOHN TURNER,
JOHN GLOVER,
CHAS. SIMPSON.

Witness to the signing of all Parties, BROADHURST HARDING.

[16] L. Jewitt, *Ceramic Art of Great Britain* (1878) ii, 186–7.
[17] *Staffordshire Advertiser*, 10 November 1804:

TO BE SOLD BY AUCTION

By Mr Cook

on the premises

At Weston Covney, in the parish of Caverswall and county of Stafford, on Tuesday the 20th & Wednesday the 21st days of November 1804.

All the FARMING STOCK, Corn, Hay, and Implements of Husbandry, together with a collection of modern and elegant HOUSEHOLD FURNITURE, belonging to WILLIAM TURNER, Esq., who is changing his residence.

The out-stock consists of four famous in-calf cows, two stirks, three calves, ten sheep, one strong draught mare, one four years old galloway, two large stacks of remarkably fine hay, one stack and a bag of oats, a quantity of unthrashed wheat, one narrow wheeled cart, land roller, ox harrow, gearing for three horses, ploughs, harrows, malt mill, one horse chaise and harness, forks, rakes, and various other farming utensils.

The Furniture comprises four-post and camp bedsteads, with Manchester stripe, printed, and bordered calico furnitures, fine feather beds, bolsters and pillows, bedside and floor carpets, Venetian stair carpet with brass rods, handsome tea room suit, consisting of eight beautiful painted chairs, with cushions stuffed with hair, and fine bordered chintz covers, sofa on socket casters, and window curtains with rich painted cornices to correspond, Turkey imitation carpet, sixteen feet by thirteen (new), two japanned firescreen poles, mahogany card and pembroke tables, beautiful Botany-Bay wood tea chest, with caddies and cut glass jar, and a painted wire fender with brass feet, balls and bottom plate; mahogany dining tables, hall lamp, mahogany and painted chairs, pier and Large swing dressing glasses, mahogany chests of drawers and bason stands, dressing tables and toilets, painted wire fenders and fire irons, plated candelsticks, oak tables and chairs, a number of excellent barrels, and a great variety of useful kitchen furniture.

The Farming Stock will be sold on the first, and the Furniture (which is elegant and nearly new) the second day; and the sale will commence each morning at ten o'clock.

[18] *Staffordshire Advertiser*, 5 April 1806.

[19] ibid.

[20] *Staffordshire Advertiser*, 12 April 1806:

JOHN GLOVER

Begs leave to inform his Friends and the Potteries in general, that he has taken to the Cart and Carrying business, of Mr Thos. COLCLOUGH, of Stone, who has declined the Carrying business.

[21] Percy Adams, *John Henry Clive*, 1947, p. 4n.

[22] loc cit.

[23] *Staffordshire Advertiser*, 16 December 1809:

NOTICE IS HEREBY GIVEN

That the Partnership heretofore subsisting between JAMES CHETHAM, & RICHARD WOOLLEY, of Lane End, in the county of Stafford, potters; and lately between ANN CHETHAM, (widow of the said James Chetham) and the said Richard Woolley, was dissolved on the eleventh day of November last. . . . And that the business is now carried on separately by the said ANN CHETHAM, at the Old Manufactory; and by the said RICHARD WOOLLEY, at the Manufactory heretofore belonging to Messrs Turners, in Lane End. Witness our hands this 12th day of December, 1809.

ANN CHETHAM
RICHARD WOOLLEY.

Signed in the
presence of
A. BARLOW.
F. EVANS.

[24] *Staffordshire Advertiser*, 5 July 1806:

BANKRUPTS

John Turner, late of Lane End, Staffordshire, potter, July 21, 22, at Trentham, and August 16, at the Dog Inn, Sandon. Attorney, Mr Tomlinson, Hanley.

William Turner, Lane End, Staffordshire, potter, June [*sic*] 21, 22, at Trentham, and August 16, at the Dog Inn, Sandon. Attorney, Mr Tomlinson, Hanley.

In the *Staffordshire Advertiser* of 30 August 1806 the following notice appeared:
The Creditors who have proved their Debts, under a Commission of Bankrupt, awarded and issued against WILLIAM TURNER, late of Lane End, in the County of Stafford, Potter, Dealer and Chapman, are desired to meet on Thursday, the 4th day of September next, at 11 o'clock in the forenoon, at the Union Hotel, in Lane End aforesaid, to take into consideration and determine upon the several matters following, namely: As to the Assignees of the said Bankrupt's Estate, being empowered to dispose of sundry Earthenware Goods and other property, part of the said Bankrupt's Estate, by Private Contract, and on Credit, and to accept Bills or Notes in payment: Also as to the measures to be pursued by the Assignees, on the part of the Estate, as to a lien claimed by a Creditor of the said Bankrupt, on his interest in a certain Farm, called Moorvill, situate in the parish of Caverswall, in the said County of Stafford;—in respect to the outstanding Debts and Effects, due or belonging to the Co-partnership of WILLIAM AND JOHN TURNER; and to the Assignees being empowered to prefer, join in, or to consent to any petition on the part of the joint Creditors, of the said William and John Turner, as Copartners, for the proof of such joint Debts, and for the Creditors at such Meeting, to assent to, or to dissent from the said Assignees, commencing, prosecuting, contesting, opposing, or defending any suit or suits, or other proceedings at law or in equity, touching or concerning all or any of the matters or things before mentioned, or in respect to any disputed account between the said Bankrupt's estate, and any person or persons, or otherwise regarding the said Bankrupt's estate, in any respect; or to the compounding, submitting to arbitration, or otherwise arranging, agreeing, compromising, settling, disposing of, or giving up the same respectively.

By Order of the Assignees.
J. TOMLINSON. Solicitor.

Hanley, 25th August 1806.

Another notice appeared in the *Staffordshire Advertiser* of 12 August 1815:

WHEREAS Mr JOHN TURNER, of Lightwood Lodge, near Lane End, in the county of Stafford, hath conveyed and assigned over his real and personal Estate, in trust, for the benefit of such of his Creditors who shall execute such Deed, on or before the first day of October next, or signify their consent thereto in writing within that period, which is requested to be sent to Mr EVANS, Attorney, in Lane End.

NOTICE IS HEREBY GIVEN,
That the said Deed now lies at the Machine Office of JOHN SMITH Esq in Lane End aforesaid, for the inspection and signatures of such of the Creditors of the said Mr Turner, who have not already executed the same; and that such of them who shall not execute such

Deed, or signify their consent thereto in writing within the time aforesaid, will be excluded all benefit arising therefrom.

7th August, 1815.

The sequel to this is seen in the *Staffordshire Advertiser* of 28 October 1815:

THE CREDITORS of Mr JOHN TURNER, late of Lightwood Lodge, who have executed the Deed of Assignment, are requested to meet the Trustee at the Crown and Anchor, in Lane End, on Thursday the 9th day of November, 1815, to take into their consideration such matters as may then be produced; at which time a statement of the accounts will be laid before them.

FRANCIS EVANS, Solicitor.

Lane-End, 26th. Oct. 1815.

In the *Staffordshire Advertiser* of 29 March 1817 the following notice was published:

Mr JOHN TURNER'S CREDITORS.

NOTICE IS HEREBY GIVEN, that a meeting of the Creditors who have signed the Trust Deed of Mr JOHN TURNER, late of Lightwood Lodge, near Lane-End, in the County of Stafford, Gentleman, will be held at the house of Mr Biddulph, at the White Lion, in Lane-End, on Saturday the 5th day of April next, at the hour of one in the afternoon, for the purpose of making oaths of their claims, if required, and of then settling the amount of the Dividend arising from the Estate and Effects of the said John Turner, and of fixing an early day for payment of the same.

26th March 1817.

On 12 April a further notice appeared:

Mr JOHN TURNER'S CREDITORS.

The Creditors of Mr JOHN TURNER, late of Lightwood Lodge, near Lane End, in the county of Stafford, Gentleman, who have executed the Deed of Trust, bearing date the 15th day of June, 1815, may receive a Dividend of 6s. 1d. in the pound upon their applying to Mr WM. LYCETT, at the Coal Weighing Machine, at Lane End aforesaid, any day (Sunday excepted) between the hours of nine o'clock in the morning, and three in the afternoon.

April 10th 1817.

[25] *Staffordshire Advertiser*, 2 August 1806:

TO BE SOLD BY AUCTION

By Mr COOK.

On the Premises, at Moorville, in the Parish of Caverswall, and county of Stafford, on Tuesday the 19th, and Wednesday the 20th of August, 1806;

All the Farming Stock, and Household Furniture, of WILLIAM TURNER Esq; the Farming Stock consists of two good saddle horses, one narrow wheeled cart, two wheel barrows, corn fan, two harrows, gearing for one horse, rakes, pikels, &c.

The Household Furniture comprises, bedsteads, with fluted, mahogany, and oak feet posts, and chintz, moreen, and other furnitures, feather beds, bolsters and pillows, mattrasses [*sic*], fine blankets, counterpanes, and cotton bed covers, bed, and table linen, chintz, dimity, and other window curtains, square and circular mahogany card, dining, and work tables, handsome mahogany side table, mahogany, painted, and stained chairs, mahogany chests of drawers, large painted wardrobe, pier glasses in gilt frames, dressing glasses, and tables, bason stands, Scotch carpet, stair carpets, and floor cloths, mahogany pole fire screens, paper, and japanned tea trays, and waiters, a capital eight days clock, dresser and shelves, polished grates, fenders, and fire irons, plated, brass, and iron candlesticks, mash tubs, barrels and brewing vessels, copper pots, kettles and stew pans, kitchen range, with various other useful kitchen requisites, a handsome Gig and harness.

The Farming Stock will be sold on the morning of the first day, and the Sale to commence at ten o'clock each morning, as the whole must be sold in two days.

[26] *Staffordshire Advertiser*, 2 August 1806:

Valuable Farming Stock and Furniture

TO BE SOLD BY AUCTION

By Mr COOK

On the premises, at Lightwood, near Lane End, in the county of Stafford, on Thursday the 21st of August, and the two following days;

All the Farming Stock, and Household Furniture of JOHN TURNER Esq. The Farming Stock consists of three good draught hourses, two saddle horses, two cows, nine pigs, twenty-six ewes and lambs, gearing for three horses, two carts, land-roller, a quantity of straw, three stone troughs, &c.

The Household Furniture comprises, mahogany and oak four post, and tent bedsteads, with chintz, cotton, moreen, and other furnitures, fine goose feather beds, bolsters and pillows, blankets, Marseilles quilts, counterpanes &c., mahogany dining, pembroke, card, and dressing tables, and stands, a beautiful cellaret, sofa with cotton cover, chintz, moreen, and other curtains, mahogany chests of drawers, bason stands, &c., handsome pier glass in gilt frame, swing dressing glasses, and boxes, mahogany, painted, and stained chairs, toilet tables and covers, Scotch and Wilton carpets, and hearth rugs, a quantity of prints in handsome frames, plated and brass candlesticks, a plated cruet frame and casters, an excellent time piece, ale, wine, and tumbler glasses, and decanters, grates, fenders, and fire irons, dresser with shelves, &c. large white table, large copper furnace, mash tubs, barrels, &c. a quantity of old and new timber, a parcel of bags, &c. handsome chaise for a pair of horses, a modern gig, with harness compleat.

The Farming Stock and carriages will be sold on the morning of the first day, and the Sale to commence at 10 o'clock each morning.

[27] The notice of this sale appeared in the *Staffordshire Advertiser*, 13 September 1806.

[28] The notice of this sale appeared in the *Staffordshire Advertiser*, 6 June 1807.

[29] The notice of this sale appeared in the *Staffordshire Advertiser*, 22 May 1813.

[30] Certain of these books may be identified:

'Montfaucon's Antiquities'—Bernard de Montfaucon, *L'Antiquité expliquée et représentée en figures*, 5 vols, Paris, 1719.

'Botanical Magazine'—published annually by William Curtis from 1787.

'Bewick's Quadrupeds'—Thomas Bewick, *A General History of Quadrupeds*, 1790.

'Grew's Anatomy of Plants'—Nathaniel Grew, *The Anatomy of Plants*, 1682.

'Beceuil'—Comte de Caylus, *Receuil d'Antiquités égyptiennes, étrusques, grecques, romaines, et gauloises*, 6 vols, 1752–5.

It is especially interesting to find mention of 'Pergolesi's Engravings' among William Turner's effects, since we know from Andrew Abbott's accounts that on 2 November 1782 J. Abbott was paid 10*s.* 6*d.* for having bought from Pergolesi '2 Numbers Engravings'. Michelangelo Pergolesi was an engraver and watercolourist of the second half of the eighteenth century. At about the age of 60, he came from Rome to London, where he worked with Adam. His principal work, *Designs for Various Ornaments* (1777–1801) influenced the art of furniture. (E. Bénézit, *Dictionnaire des Peintres, Sculpteurs, Dessinateurs et Graveurs*, 1953 edn, p. 596.)

[31] The notice of this sale appeared in the *Staffordshire Advertiser* of 16 September 1815.

[32] loc. cit.

[33] loc. cit.

[34] *Pottery Mercury*, 7 July 1824:

'Died. On Saturday week, aged 57, John Turner, Esq, of Brewood Hall.'

[35] L. Jewitt, *Ceramic Art of Great Britain* (1878), ii, 265.

[36] See William White, *History, Gazeteer and Directory of Staffordshire* (1834), p. 571.

[37] *Staffordshire Advertiser*, 11 July 1835.

CHAPTER TEN

The Industrial Revolution

LOOKING AT THE VAST congeries of potworks in Stoke-on-Trent today, it is difficult to conceive of a time when Staffordshire was not associated with potting. Yet this was the case as late as 1769, when P. Russell, in his *England Displayed*, wrote of Staffordshire: 'The principal manufactures of this county are cloth and iron utensils, all kinds of which are made here in great perfection'[1]—without a mention of pots. Later still, in 1839, the obituary of the Turners' modeller, William Massey, said that '*In the infancy of potting*, he contributed in a considerable degree by his well-known talents to the advancement of this beautiful portion of our national industry.'[2] Allowing for the hyperbole natural to obituarists, this writer must have thought of potting as a recent innovation in Staffordshire.

So, as an industry, it was. The Turner factory at Lane End was founded about 1759 and came to an end in 1829. These dates coincide almost exactly with those traditionally accepted as convenient limits of the Industrial Revolution—1760 to 1830. During that period the Potteries changed from a haphazard collection of family businesses conducted in rustic potworks to an industry centralized in the Five Towns. The factory built by Thomas and John Wedgwood was the first un-thatched potbank in Staffordshire.[3] The new factories were at first disembowelled Georgian houses, such as Shelton Hall (Plate 35), leased by John Turner I in 1779—the kind of building which seemed impossibly elegant and archaic to Bennett's Edwin Clayhanger:

> Mr Orgreave crossed the road and then stood still to gaze at the façade of the Sytch Pottery. It was a long two-storey building, purest Georgian, of red brick with very elaborate stone facings which contrasted admirably with the austere simplicity of the walls. The porch was lofty, with a majestic flight of steps narrowing to the doors. The ironwork of the basement railings was unusually rich and impressive.
>
> 'Ever seen another pot-works like that?' demanded Mr Orgreave, enthusiastically musing.
>
> 'No' said Edwin. Now that the question was put to him, he never *had* seen another potworks like that.[4]

In other ways, the Potteries exhibited very clearly the familiar hall-marks of the Industrial Revolution. There was a rapid increase in population. In Lane End and Longton together, it rose from 1,300 in 1762 to 9,608 in 1831. As in the textile, iron, and coal industries, new machinery revolutionized production. Grinding with a horse-gin mill, such as Thomas Wedgwood left to his wife in his will, was found inadequate for large quantities of raw materials, and in the second half of the seventeenth century watermills and windmills were adapted for grinding flint and stones. These, too, had their disadvantages. Watermills could only be used with a good supply of water; windmills were at the mercy of the weather.

It seems probable that John Turner pioneered the use of Newcomen's fire engine to pump water back over a water-wheel. When Wedgwood and Turner visited Cornwall in 1775 they saw tin-mines where the Savery improved fire engine of Newcomen was used to pump water from the pits. They saw how this water, pumped by fire engine, was shot over water-wheels to work 'stamping' machines. These tin-ore stamping machines would suggest the possibility of using a fire engine for raising water over a wheel.

> Mr Turner [wrote Shaw] . . . erected in the open ground before his manufactory, a machine by which he could turn his throwing engine and lathes. This was open to the inspection of all the potters of the time; but no application of the principle was made, until after steam engines were introduced; as by Mr Wedgwood, and Mr Spode.[5]

In a rough manuscript (*circa* 1782) discovered by Dr John Thomas pinned to the drawings of Portfolio 97 of the Watt MSS. in the Birmingham Public Library, Josiah Wedgwood tells James Watt that 'If in your Road [you] may see Mr Turner's Mill at Lane Delph'. It may be that this is a slip for Lane End, or that Turner actually had his grinding-mill at Lane Delph. In the same letter Wedgwood records that 'Mr Spode of Stoke has a fire engine to raise ▽ [water] to work a Wheel'.

The fire engine was costly in its consumption of fuel, and so capricious that in some areas it was known as a 'whimsey'. As Josiah Wedgwood attended meetings of the Lunar Society at Birmingham, of which Matthew Boulton was a member, it was only a matter of time before the steam engine was introduced at Etruria. In 1784 one of the Boulton Sun and Planet engines was erected there to drive the clay mill, the flint mill, and the smaller colour-grinding pans. In 1793 a second engine was installed. Other potters who acquired steam engines, some from 'pirate' manufacturers, were Thomas Wolfe and his son-in-law Robert Hamilton, Enoch Wood, William Adams, E. Keeling, Josiah Spode II, and Thomas Minton.

The introduction of steam power hastened the replacement of wood and charcoal, as a firing fuel, by coal, though this had already begun. In 1753 Henry

Delamain, a Dublin potter, had petitioned the English Parliament for a reward for having fired delft ware with coals 'as well as was ever done with turf and wood'. He was, in fact, granted £1,000 by the Irish Parliament, but the English were unimpressed, as coal firing was already in practice in England: an engraving of the Worcester porcelain factory in the *Gentleman's Magazine* of 1752 showed 'the yard for coal'.[6] For certain pastes—Champion's porcelain, for example—wood was retained, as coal would have spoilt them. Shaw states that 'William Littler of Brownhills about 1765 was manager of a porcelain manufactory in Shelton for Baddeley & Fletcher . . . they fired with wood because the body would not bear coals'.[7] Gerverot's porcelain may well have required the same delicate treatment, but in the firing of pottery coal superseded wood as the staple fuel, and in 1785 John Turner became a member of a 'coal ring' presided over by Josiah Wedgwood.[8]

It was the incidence of coal which determined the geographical situation of the Potteries. But the potters also needed to import flints and clay into the Potteries, and to send out their wares to London and other ports. When Turner first arrived at Lane End the only means of transport was by road, and the condition of the roads was appalling. In 1768 Arthur Young wrote of the main road from Knutsford to Newcastle:

> A more dreadful road cannot be imagined and wherever the country is the least sandy the pavement is discontinued and the ruts and holes most execrable. I was forced to hire two men at one place to support my chaise from overthrowing in turning but for a cart of goods overthrown and almost buried. Let me persuade all travellers to avoid this terrible country. . . .[9]

For potters, transporting fragile wares, the uneven roads were a particular hazard: we recall the two crates of Turner ware which failed to reach the Fleet Street showrooms. The remedy was to set up turnpike trusts by acts of parliament, by which local men of substance undertook the repair and upkeep of tracts of road, recouping themselves by levying tolls on travellers. The first road to be turnpiked near the Potteries was in 1714, on 'the eight computed miles from Tittensor to Talk o' the Hill on the port road from London to some of the northern parts of the kingdom'. In 1759, as we have seen, John Turner became a trustee for the Staffordshire area of the road from Derby to Newcastle-under-Lyme. This road enabled the potters to take their wares to Uttoxeter market, and to bring back flints and clay from Wellington Ferry as return loads in the wagons which took their wares consigned to Hull by the Trent Navigation at that point.

After about 1765 the concern with roads gave place to a new interest, the construction of canals. James Brindley lived near the Potteries at Leek, and frequently met Josiah Wedgwood. Earl Gower, Wedgwood's patron and 'unfailing friend', was a brother-in-law of the canal-building Duke of Bridgwater. In view of the potters' need for a smooth form of transport, Staffordshire was an obvious starting-point for canal schemes. In 1765 John Turner subscribed three guineas towards obtaining an Act of Parliament for making a canal from the Trent at Wilden in Derbyshire to the Mersey.[10] The secretaries of this undertaking were Thomas Whieldon and Josiah Wedgwood. Its result was the building of the Grand Trunk Canal, which ran right through the Potteries and connected Liverpool and Hull. Already, in 1759, a canal had joined Stoke to Newcastle. In 1773 the Caldon Canal linked Stretton, Leek, and Frogshall. Frogshall and Uttoxeter were joined in 1797, and in the same year extensions of the Grand Trunk gave access from Longport to Burslem, Shelton to Cobridge, and from Stoke to Lane End. The Newcastle Junction Canal was built in 1798.

The age of canal transport was succeeded by an age of railway transport, and although the period of railway building lies largely outside the period of the Turner factory, it is worth noting that when, in 1806, the old Lane End factory was sold up, one of the chief advantages claimed for it was 'the ready delivery of Coals, by a Railway, within 40 yards of the Pit's Mouth.'[11]

The transport revolution produced a corresponding revolution in marketing methods. In the seventeenth and early eighteenth centuries most wares were sold through travelling salesmen—as Dr Plot called them, 'the poor Crate-men who carry them [the pots] at their backs, all over the country'.[12] This method persisted: as late as 1785 the Staffordshire potters collectively resisted the Government's proposal to abolish pedlars and hawkers, and a Cruikshank engraving of 1797 shows 'Itinerant Dealers in Staffordshire Ware' on the Road to Lichfield.[13] But as the roads improved so did the possibility of transporting large consignments of pottery to London warehouses, to the showrooms of the potters themselves, such as Wedgwood's rooms in Greek Street and Turner and Abbott's in Fleet Street, or to 'china men' like Clark Durnford.

Turner's altruism in placing his fire engine on general view was a characteristic expression of that disdain for monopolies which was part of the credo of the Industrial Revolution. In opposing the extension of Champion's patent in 1775, Wedgwood wrote:

> When Mr Wedgwood discovered the art of making *Queen's Ware*, which employs ten times more people than all the china works in the kingdom, he did not ask for a patent for this important discovery. A patent would greatly have limited its public utility. Instead of *one hundred manufactories* of Queen's Ware, there would have been *one*;

and instead of an exportation to all parts of the world, a few pretty things would have been made for the amusement of the people of fashion in England.[14]

The question of monopolies is, of course, allied to the question of plagiarism, especially relevant to any study of the Turners, so often dismissed as 'imitators' of Wedgwood. Wedgwood's pronouncements on the subject of imitation were defiantly liberal.

So far from being afraid of other People getting our patterns, [he wrote to Bentley in 1769] we should Glory in it, throw out all the hints we can & if possible have all the Artists in Europe working after our models. . . . With respect to myself, there is nothing relating to business I so much wish for as being released from these degrading slavish chains, these mean selfish fears of other people copying my works.[15]

And again, four days later:

With respect to *Rivalship*, we will cast all dread of that behind our backs, treat it as a base, & vanquished enemy, & not bestow another serious thought upon it.[16]

These remarks seem a little disingenuous in the light of his order to Bentley a month later to 'Say nothing of the Br——ze *Encaustic* to anybody';[17] the lawsuit he took against Humphrey Palmer for invading his pattern patent; and the almost pathological security which prevailed at Etruria.[18] Wedgwood was by nature a jealous creator; and where there was a conflict between the liberal and the businessman, the latter usually won. But at least, as far as we know, his cordiality towards Turner was never disturbed by complaints of imitation. Indeed, the boot may sometimes have been on the other foot: Shaw tells us that 'Mr Wedgwood's encaustic painting was in imitation of Messrs Turner's on white body porcelain'.[19]

In labour relations, too, Wedgwood the sympathizer with revolutionaries was overriden by Wedgwood the captain of industry. In 1772, when his workmen refused to start work until their rates of pay had been settled, he did not scruple to threaten them with mass sackings—'I told them we could make a new sett of hands, which they must be sensible was in my power to do.'[20] But in the next century the pottery workers' discontent was to take a form which no one man, however formidable, could allay or quash. Because of their geographical situation, half-way between Manchester and Birmingham, and on the direct route to London, the Potteries were a favourite halting-place for political reform agitators such as representatives of Orator Hunt. William Massey, the Turners' modeller, was sworn in as a special constable for Burslem in 1817.[21] The Hanley registers, which record the deaths of Broadhurst Harding and Fidellé Duvivier, were damaged in Chartist riots.

For these disturbances the Methodists were partly, and sometimes justly, blamed. As in the other industrial areas, Nonconformity was strong in the Potteries. Wesley was idolized: there is no one so much portrayed in busts and medallions. The most popular and successful of the busts is that by Enoch Wood, to whom Wesley gave a sitting when he stayed in Wood's house. There is a marked Turner medallion of Wesley in blue jasper in the Museum of Fine Arts, Boston, and another was sold at Puttick and Simpson's auction rooms on 13 May 1958. The demand for portraits of Wesley was so great that when he visited Wednesbury effigies of him were made by painting the cervicles of horses to resemble the cravated preacher.[22] 'At the southern extremity [of the Foley]', wrote Shaw, 'are the House and Factory of the late Mr Myatt; one of the first persons who received the Wesleyan Methodist preachers; and in whose parlour the late Rev. J. Wesley stood, while from the window he preached to a vast congregation, when last he passed thro' Staffordshire only a few months prior to his decease.'[23] The founder of primitive Methodism was a potter, William Clowes. One of Turner's business associates, James Neale, married Elizabeth Simpson, the sister of a notorious Nonconformist preacher of Brewood, and contributed money for the foundation of a chapel at Brewood.[24] Job Ridgway (1759–1813), son of Ralph Ridgway of Chell, the potter, divided his time between acting as a Wesleyan missionary and working as a journeyman potter in Hanley.

The changes in the potting industry should be seen against the background of a quite exceptional expansion of demand. This was largely a reflection of changes in taste and social habits, which in part, at any rate, were unconnected with the Industrial Revolution. For the potters, the most significant development was the rapid growth of tea consumption. In the early eighteenth century tea-drinking was virtually confined to the aristocracy and 'middling classes'. In the course of the century, however, the duty on tea was drastically reduced and the price fell by almost 90 per cent; and by 1800 it had largely replaced milk and beer as the main drink of the working classes. To a lesser extent the pottery industry benefited from the rise in coffee- and chocolate-drinking, which, fostered no doubt by the growth of coffee-houses and clubs, became increasingly fashionable among the well-to-do. There was also a rise in the consumption of hot cooked meals.

The industry's main competitor, pewter, was unsuitable for hot food and beverages, being a good conductor of heat. In any case, its price was rising, partly as a result of the rigid selling conditions of the Pewterers' Guild, but mainly because of the shortage of tin and lead. When Turner and Wedgwood visited Cornwall in 1775 they were warned that the tin-miners might attack them, though, in fact, this did not happen.[25]

The growth of the home market, stimulated by the rise in population and national income, was complemented by an increased export trade. In 1765 Wedgwood wrote to his friend Sir William Meredith—perhaps with some exaggeration:

'The bulk of our particular manufacture is exported to foreign markets; for our home consumption is very trifling compared with what is sent abroad.'[26] The majority of exports went to Europe. France was a particularly vulnerable market, for although the aristocratic porcelain of Sèvres had attained a quality which Derby, for all the braggadocio of its crossed batons, could never hope to rival, French pottery for domestic use was far inferior to that of Wedgwood and Turner. This explains the interest taken by the English potters in the negotiations leading up to the Eden treaty, an interest amply justified by the expansion of trade which followed its conclusion. Exports of earthenware to France are estimated to have risen from 256,575 pieces in 1785 to 3,167,854 pieces in 1789. The Turners benefited especially from the growth of export trade, and were correspondingly hard hit by the Revolution which nullified the Eden treaty.

The genius of the Industrial Revolution in the Potteries was Josiah Wedgwood. It was Wedgwood who introduced steam power, and developed the idea of the division of labour in the potworks, trained women, founded a school of trainee artists, banned drinking, insisted on cleanliness and enforced punctuality by a primitive clocking-in system.[27] It was Wedgwood who did the missionary work for the Grand Trunk Canal, who organized the opposition to Champion and formed the General Chamber of Manufacturers of Great Britain, a national body through which he hoped to influence Government policy.

But it is not merely by studying this man, a Fellow of the Royal Society and a demi-millionaire, that we shall understand the course of the Industrial Revolution in the Potteries. In historian's jargon, he was more a 'cause' than an 'effect', more an industrialist than a potter.

Do you think my friend [he wrote to Bentley] that the outline of a Jug, even a Boling-broke, or the fine turn of a teapot are synonims to Creating a River, or building a City? No, no, my friend, let us speak softly, or rather be silent on such Fribbling performances, your friend shall endeavour to please the Ladys . . . but he must not be vain of such trifles, & mistake them for great actions.[28]

And on another occasion, writing to Bentley on the subject of canals, he asked:

How shall I descend from these elevated subjects down to *pots* and *pipkins*?[29]

That sentence fixes the difference between Wedgwood and Turner. For to John Turner and William, his son, the pots and pipkins were all that mattered, and canals and grand associations were only a means to an end. Wedgwood was almost contemptuous of the craft by which he made his fortune. The Turners, from all we learn of them, seem to have been completely dedicated to the craft, without the imagination to look beyond it which might have brought them final success and made this book the corrective to a succession of Victorian eulogies.

NOTES TO CHAPTER TEN

[1] P. Russell, *England Displayed* (1769), ii, 65.

[2] *Staffordshire Advertiser*, 30 March 1839.

[3] W. Parson and T. Bradshaw, *Staffordshire General and Commercial Directory for 1818*, p. xlix.

[4] Arnold Bennett, *Clayhanger* (Penguin edn), p. 121.

[5] Simeon Shaw, *History of the Staffordshire Potteries* (1829), p. 173.

[6] *Gentleman's Magazine* (1752), p. 348.

[7] Simeon Shaw, *History of the Staffordshire Potteries* (1829), p. 199.

[8] Wedgwood MSS. Commonplace Book, p. 210. The list of members is transcribed by Dr John Thomas, *The Economic Development of the North Staffordshire Potteries since 1730, with Special Reference to the Industrial Revolution* (unpublished thesis, London University Library), p. 334.

[9] Arthur Young, *Tour Through the North of England* (1768), iii, 433.

[10] Dr John Thomas, *The Economic Development of the North Staffordshire Potteries since 1730, with Special Reference to the Industrial Revolution*, Appendix xix, p. 987.

[11] *Staffordshire Advertiser*, 19 April 1806.

[12] Dr Robert Plot, *History of Staffordshire* (1686), p. 124.

[13] Illustrated by Arthur Hayden, *Spode and His Successors* (1925), opp. p. 6.

[14] Quoted, Hugh Owen, *Two Centuries of Ceramic Art in Bristol*, 1873, p. 132.

[15] Wedgwood to Bentley, 27 September 1769. (*Letters of Josiah Wedgwood 1762–1772*, ed. Lady Farrer, 1903, pp. 290–291.)

[16] Wedgwood to Bentley, 1 October 1769. (*Letters of Josiah Wedgwood, 1762–1772*, ed. Lady Farrer, 1903, p. 298.)

[17] Wedgwood to Bentley, 30 October 1769. (ibid., p. 305.)

[18] See Eliza Meteyard, *Life of Wedgwood*, 1866, ii, 333n.

[19] Simeon Shaw, *History of the Staffordshire Potteries* (1829), p. 204.

[20] Undated, but the postmark appears to be 22 July 1772. Wedgwood MSS. E.18381–25, quoted by Dr John Thomas, *The Economic Development of the North Staffordshire Potteries since 1730, with Special Reference to the Industrial Revolution* (unpublished thesis, London University Library), p. 540.

[21] See Dr John Thomas, ibid., fig. 18 at p. 571.

[22] There is one such effigy at Rousham House, Oxfordshire, and a more finished example is in the author's possession. See also *The Countryman*, vol xlii, no 2. Winter 1950, p. 393.

[23] Simeon Shaw, *History of the Staffordshire Potteries* (1829), p. 72.

[24] 'May 3, 1803, a small neat chapel was opened at *Brewood*, in Staffordshire. The whole expense of which is from the kind benevolence of a friend in London, whose partner in life is a native of the place.' (*The Evangelical Magazine*, 1803, p. 271.)
'In 1800 John Simpson, the parish clerk there [Brewood], resigned that office, and in the hope of finding something more satisfying than the doctrine of the parish church, secured a certificate for a cottage in his possession. There he arranged for the holding of services, frequently conducted by two of the Wolverhampton ministers. Such conduct was not allowed to pass unopposed, and an attempt was made to suppress the meeting by summoning him before the magistrates for holding an "unlawful assembly". This charge Simpson rebutted by producing his certificate. Thereafter a chapel was erected, and opened on May 3 1803, thanks to the generosity of James Neale, of St Paul's Churchyard, London, a prominent Evangelical layman, at one time treasurer of the London Itinerant Society, who had married Mr Simpson's sister.' (A. G. Matthews, *The Congregational Churches of Staffordshire*, 1924, p. 178.)

[25] *Proceedings* of the Wedgwood Society, No 2 (1957), p. 83.

[26] Quoted by Dr John Thomas, *The Economic Development of the North Staffordshire Potteries since 1730, with Special Reference to the Industrial Revolution*, pp. 782–3.

[27] Neil McKendrick, 'Josiah Wedgwood and Factory Discipline', *Proceedings* of the Wedgwood Society, No. 5 (1963) p. 2.

[28] Wedgwood to Bentley, 2 March 1767. (*Letters of Josiah Wedgwood, 1762–1772*, ed. Lady Farrer, 1903, p. 123.)

[29] Wedgwood to Bentley, 27 February 1780. (*Letters of Josiah Wedgwood, 1772–1780.* ed. Lady Farrer, 1903, p. 452.)

Index

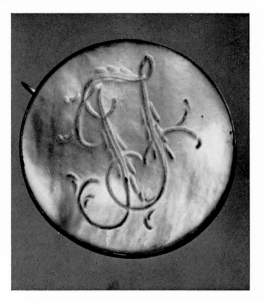

1a John Turner I, from a blue jasper plaque, mounted during the late nineteenth century, in white parian. (Mrs Eric Young)

1b Mother-o'-pearl button from a coat of John Turner I, carved in relief with the initials 'J.T.' (Miss Fanny Turner)

1c Brewood Hall, Staffordshire. (See pp. 1–2.) Photograph taken by courtesy of Mr C. O. Langley

2a *The Degg Teapot. Dated March 1762. The legend round the base reads: LORD TRENTHAM WITH HIS FRENCH DOLLS. Mark TURNER impressed. (See pp. 12–13.) (Whereabouts unknown. Photograph copied from* The Connoisseur *of May 1907, by kind permission of the Editor)*

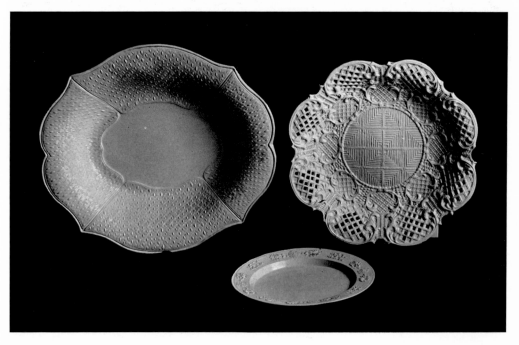

2b *Three moulded saltglaze plates, perhaps from the factory of Turner and Banks. Unmarked. (See pp. 4–5.) (Mrs Eric Young)*

3a *Blue jasper cup and saucer, and blue and black jasper scent bottle with silver cap. All marked TURNER impressed. (See p. 17) (Royal Scottish Museum, Edinburgh)*

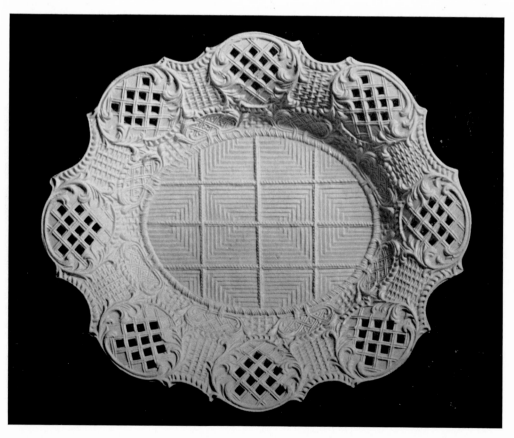

3b *A moulded saltglaze plate, perhaps from the factory of Turner and Banks. Unmarked. (Mrs Eric Young)*

4b *Blue jasper sucrier and cover. Mark TURNER impressed. (Mrs Eric Young)*

4a *Blue jasper coffee pot and cover. Mark TURNER impressed. (Mrs Eric Young)*

5a *Three blue jasper vases. Mark TURNER impressed. (Mrs Eric Young)*

5b *Two fern pots. That on the left is of white stoneware; that on the right,
of blue jasper. Both marked TURNER impressed. (Mrs Eric Young)*

6 *Part of a tea service of blue jasper. Marks* TURNER *and* TURNER & CO. *(James
Graham & Sons, New York)*

7 *Brooch and earrings with pendants, all of blue
jasper with ormolu mounting. (See p. 52.)
(Mrs Eric Young)*

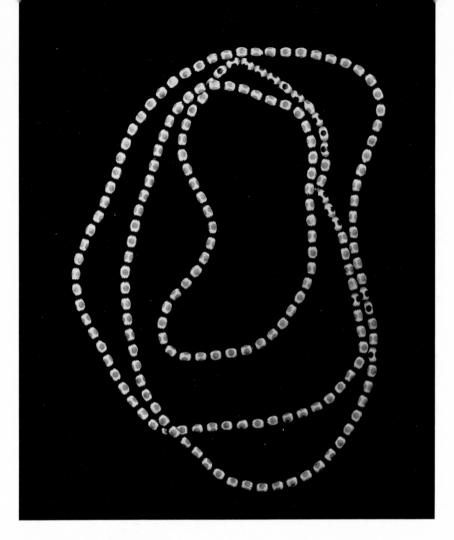

8a and b *Two necklaces of blue and black jasper. (See p. 52) (Mrs Eric Young)*

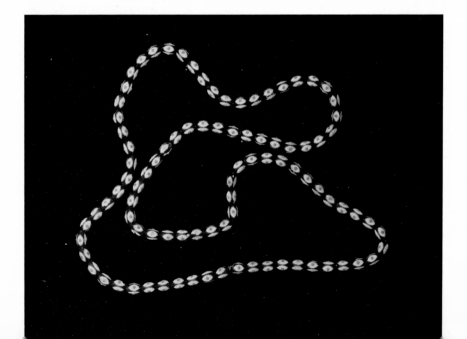

9a Black basalt teapot of silver pattern with lion knop. Mark TURNER impressed. (See p. 15) (Mrs Patrick Ogilvie)

9b Black basalt inkstand and coffee pot. Both marked TURNER impressed. (Sotheby & Co.)

10a Black basalt candlestick. Mark TURNER impressed. (See pp. 15– 16.) (Victoria and Albert Museum)

10b Black basalt bust of Matthew Prior. Mark TURNER impressed. (See pp. 15–16.) (Mrs Eric Young)

11 Cane ware coffee pot. Mark TURNER impressed. (T. W. Atkinson, Esq.)

12 *White stoneware beaker and stand. Mark TURNER impressed. (Mrs Eric Young)*

'*One cup made by them for the late Viscount Creamhorn (sic: Cremorne), has never been equalled in the district; tho' formed of the common Clay of Lane End. This was once produced by the late Jacob Warburton, Esq. at a meeting of Potters, to shew to what a degree of perfection even common pottery may be carried. It became so estimable in the opinion of its owner, that to prevent the possibility of injury, he had a proper sized mahogany box made for its reception, and in the door is a pane of glass, thro' which alone he permits it to be inspected.*' (*Simeon Shaw,* History of the Staffordshire Potteries, *1829, p. 222.*)

13a Uncle Toby (mould). Mark TURNER impressed. (See p. 18.) (Copeland-Spode factory museum, Stoke-on-Trent)

13b The Toper (mould). Mark TURNER impressed. (See p. 18.) (Copeland-Spode factory museum, Stoke-on-Trent)

14a Silver tankard with applied hoops, 1772. Louisa Courtauld and George Cowles. (Courtesy of the Ashmolean Museum, Oxford)

14b White stoneware mug with brown-painted hoops c.1790. Mark TURNER impressed. (Author's collection)

'Hooped pots. *Drinking pots at one time were made with hoops, that when two or more drank from the same tankard no one of them should take more than his share. Jack Cade promises his followers that "seven half-penny loaves shall be sold for a penny; the three-hooped pot shall have ten hoops; and I will make it felony to drink small beer."'* (Dr E. Cobham Brewer, Dictionary of Phrase and Fable)

15 *White stoneware mug, moulded with 'The Archery Lesson' and with brown-painted hoops. The silver rim bears the London date mark for 1794. Mark TURNER impressed. (See pp. 18 and 60.) (Author's collection)*

*16a Detail of moulding from a white stone-
ware jug. Mark TURNER impressed.
(James Wylde, Esq.)*

*16b White stoneware teapot painted with landscapes in blue.
Mark TURNER impressed. (Sotheby & Co.)*

17a The audience of a cock-fight (mould). Mark TURNER impressed. (Copeland-Spode factory museum, Stoke-on-Trent) (See p. 10)

17b Three stoneware jugs, moulded with (left to right) the cock fight, cherubs, and 'The Archery Lesson'. All marked TURNER impressed. (See p. 10.) (Norman Stretton Esq.)

17c Cherubs (mould). Mark TURNER impressed (Compare with Plate 26b.) (Copeland-Spode factory museum, Stoke-on-Trent)

18a White stoneware figures: the child seasons. All marked TURNER impressed. (See p. 37.) (F. A. Hopkins, Esq., The East Gate Gallery, Oxford.)

18b and c. A set of porcelain seasons modelled for the Bristol factory by Pierre Stephan. (See p. 37) (Victoria and Albert Museum)

19a Self-portrait plaque in white stoneware by William Massey. Inscribed on reverse: '14 Oct. 1835 Wm Masey alias Poor Pilgarlic. This portrait of himself was executed by the author in the sixtieth year of his practice as a Modeller and presented to E. Jones.' (See p. 25.) (Geoffrey Godden, Esq.)

19b White stoneware figure group: the parson and clerk. Mark TURNER impressed. Probably modelled by William Massey. (See p. 25.) (Tilley & Co., Antiques)

20a Cane ware teapot moulded to simulate cane-stalks. Mark *TURNER* impressed. (*Victoria and Albert Museum*)

20b Cane ware mug moulded with cherubs after a Wedgwood design, the inner rim enamelled in pink, green and blue. Mark *TURNER* impressed. (*Miss Fanny Turner*)

20c Cane ware jug moulded with Chinese scenes. Mark *TURNER* impressed. (*Author's collection*)

21a Cane ware basket and stand modelled to simulate osiers. Mark TURNER impressed. (See p. 17.) (Mrs Eric Young)

21b Cane ware dish and cover moulded to simulate pie-crust. Mark TURNER impressed. (See pp. 17 and 19.) (City Museum, Stoke-on-Trent)

22 *Cane ware bulb holder enamelled in blue. Mark* TURNER *impressed.*
(Alexandre Raghinsky, Antiques)

23 *White stoneware bust of Joseph Addison on a black basalt plinth. The name*
of the subject is impressed on the back of the bust; the plinth bears the latest
mark of the factory, the TURNER & CO *mark from which the '& CO' has*
been only partially erased. (Author's collection)

24a *White stoneware plate, transfer-printed in blue with
a version of the willow pattern containing an elephant
with a twisted trunk. Mark TURNER impressed.
(Author's collection)*

24b *White stoneware plate, transfer-printed with the willow
pattern. Mark* TURNER
MIST SOLE AGENT *impressed.
(See pp. 65–66.) (Author's collection)*

*25a White stoneware vase with brown enamelling.
Mark, J. Mist 82 Fleet Street London, impressed.
(See pp. 65–66.) (Mr and Mrs J. K. des Fontaines)*

*25b Tinted drawing of No. 82 Fleet Street by James
Findlay, c. 1845. (See p. 66.) (Guildhall Library)*

26a *White stoneware sucrier and teapot with brown enamelling. Mark TURNER impressed. (Mrs Eric Young)*

26b *White stoneware loving-cup, enamelled in brown. Compare the moulded cupids with those of Plate 17c. Mark TURNER impressed. (Mrs Eric Young)*

26c *White stoneware jug. Mark TURNER impressed. (Mrs Eric Young)*

27a Creamware plate enamelled with the arms of Thomas Giffard and Charlotte, second daughter of Viscount Courtenay, 1788. Mark TURNER 2 impressed. (See pp. 12 and 60.) (Donald Towner, Esq.)

27b Creamware plate, enamelled in brown and black with the crest of the Rasdall family. Mark TURNER impressed. (See pp. 59–60.) (Author's collection)

28a Worcester porcelain plate, painted in Tournai style in the centre in carmine, perhaps by Fidellé Duvivier, the border with five carmine flower-sprays by the Painter of the Tulip with Divergent Petals. (See p. 30.) (Sotheby & Co.)

28b Pearl ware plate, possibly decorated by the Painter of the Tulip with Divergent Petals. Mark TURNER impressed. (See p. 30.) (National Museum of Ireland, Dublin)

28c Pearl ware teapot, possibly decorated by the Painter of the Tulip with Divergent Petals. Mark TURNER impressed. (Compare with colour plate III, and see p. 30) (Author's collection)

29b Pattern 24 from the Abbott-Turner pattern book. (See p. 60.) (Mrs Constance Hare)

29a Patterns 15 and 16 from the Abbott-Turner pattern book. (See p. 60.) (Mrs Constance Hare)

30 *Pattern 26 from the Abbott-Turner pattern book. (See p. 60.) (Mrs Constance Hare)*

31a Creamware mug, unmarked but probably by
Turner, decorated with pattern 26 and husk
border. (See p. 60.) (A. T. Morley Hewitt, Esq.)

31b Inside the creamware mug, showing the modelled
frog. (A. T. Morley Hewitt, Esq.)

32a *Pearl ware drug jars. Mark* TURNER *impressed.* (*Norman Stretton Esq.*)

32b *Pearl ware tureen, cover and ladle, with blue enamelling. Mark* TURNER *impressed.* (*Victoria and Albert Museum*)

*33a Dutch-decorated cream ware plate: the Prodigal
Son in eighteenth-century dress. Mark TURNER
impressed. (See p. 20.) (National Museum of
Wales, Cardiff)*

*...m ware plate, of the type sold
...the shrine at Kevelaar. Mark
...(See p. 20.) (Donald Towner, Esq.)*

34a *Mug of soft-paste porcelain, ascribed to John Turner I by the late W. B. Honey. Decorated with Chinese scenes in underglaze blue. Mark TURNER impressed. (See p. 36.) (City Museum, Stoke-on-Trent)*

34b *The Gerverot Beaker, showing the throwing wheel. A hooped mug (cf. Plate 14b) stands on the lowest shelf. (Compare with frontispiece, and see Chapter Six.) (Antique Porcelain Company)*

34c *Hard-paste porcelain bowl, dated July 1787 and decorated by Fidellé Duvivier in sepia. (See pp. 44–45.) (British Museum)*

35 *The New Hall China Manufactory, Staffordshire, 1813, a pottery model. (See pp. 37–
38, and 40.) (George Eyre Stringer, Esq.)*

36 *Left, the type of Chinese porcelain plate from which the design of the marked Turner's Patent plate, right, was probably copied. (See p. 21–22.) (Author's collection)*

37 A part service of Turner's Patent ware, showing representative shapes. Mark Turner's Patent in red. (See pp. 21–22.) (Godden of Worthing, Ltd.)

38 *Creamware plate decorated with 'reversible heads'. Mark TURNER impressed.*
(See pp. 20–21.) (E. Coulson, Brighton)

39 *William Turner of Lane End (1762–1835). Stoneware*
bust by George Ray. Inscribed on back 'G. Ray.
Modeler (sic) Lane End.' (See pp. 25–27.) (City Museum,
Stoke-on-Trent)

40 Mrs Eric Young, great granddaughter of William Turner, at Stoneyfields, Newcastle-under-Lyme. (Photograph by Eric Plunkett)